"In this book, Staub reminds us that to transform ourselves requires self-knowledge and the wisdom to separate the true from the false in ourselves: love from emotion, vulnerability from weakness, joy from sentiment, inner peace from detachment. *The 7 Acts of Courage* accomplishes the crucial work of bringing spiritual values and psychological understanding into the marketplace of business and daily life. It is a lucid and moving invitation for each of us to live heroic lives distinguished by excellence at every level."

—*Richard Moss, M.D., author of* The "I" That Is "We", The Second Miracle, *and* The Black Butterfly

"*The 7 Acts of Courage* definitely brings more heart into the workplace and reminds us that it takes courage to act, to live, to love, and to lead by example."

—*Dan Millman, best-selling author of* Way of the Peaceful Warrior *and* Everyday Enlightenment

"*The 7 Acts of Courage* represents a leap of faith and an opportunity to reconnect to our true selves. Staub's unique approach applies the power of dreams, visions, confrontations, and vulnerability to restore our courage to move and act in decisive, ethical patterns."

-*Lee W. Kinard, Jr., Ed.D., retired news anchor, WFMY-TV (CBS), Greensboro, North Carolina*

"Robert Staub's *The 7 Acts of Courage* supplies tools that have allowed me to take a more introspective look at life and enhance my leadership and personal growth. He affirms that success or failure in life is totally up to me, based on my ability to find and apply courage."

—*Edward M. Gabriel, United States Ambassador to Morocco*

"This book provides the missing piece between knowing in my heart *what* I need to do and discovering *how* to do it. I recommend it to anyone ready to discover the next level of meaning in life."

—*Annette Simmons, author of* Territorial Games *and president of Group Process Consulting*

"This book is so delightful and easy to read. Through the authentic voice of Dusty Staub come compelling stories, pragmatic tools, courageous inspiration, and centered guidance. Life again sings, and so will you as you read this remarkable book."

—*Jane Penland Hoover, president and CEO, PenStorkes, and former president and CEO, Clairmont Oaks*

"Every once in a while, a book comes along that touches your soul, moves you, and helps you grow. . . . You're holding that book in your hands now: It will help you open your heart to exercise greater courage, to view your life's potential, and to fulfill the purpose of your soul."

—*Dave Richards, Ph.D., director, UK product marketing, Nortel*

"For those who wish to live a balanced, healthy, and happy life, this results-oriented yet loving book provides a structure for action, and a method for finding more fulfilling personal relationships and a more productive work life. It shows that only the individual has the power to initiate changes that ultimately result in lasting happiness."

—*Richard H. Rosenzweig, partner, Alcalde & Fay, and former Chief of Staff, U.S. Department of Energy (1993-96)*

"While others provide 'soup' for the soul, Staub not only succeeds in providing a balanced meal, he supplies the recipe! This work poignantly illustrates the acts of courage required to define who we are and to discover the difference we can make if we put forth the effort to try."

—*Bill Casale, COO, Echevarria, McCalla, Raymer, Barrett & Frappier, Attorneys-at-Law*

"*The 7 Acts of Courage* unfolds into a masterful, self-directed voyage to the center of your being. I personally have used these truths to approach my potential, resulting in greater self-esteem, healing relationships, and a previously unknown appreciation of our power to love and grow."

—*Russ Moon, COO, Hickory Brands*

THE
ACTS
OF
7
COURAGE

BOLD LEADERSHIP FOR A WHOLEHEARTED LIFE

BY ROBERT E. STAUB II

Staub Leadership Publishing
166B Thatcher Rd.
Greensboro, NC 27409
Phone: (336) 282-0282
Fax: (336) 282-6013
Web: www.staubleadership.com

Ordering Information
Individual Sales: Staub Leadership Solutions products are available through most bookstores. They can also be ordered directly from Staub Leadership Solutions at the address above.
Quantity Sales: Staub Leadership Solutions products are available at special quantity discounts when purchased in bulk by corporations, associations, libraries, and others, or for college textbook/course adoptions. Please write to the address above or call Staub Leadership Solutions at 336/282-0282.

Second Edition
Printed in the United States of America
10
ISBN 0-9715850-1-6

DEDICATION

This book is dedicated to seven courageous people who inspired and helped shape my life and the lives of many others:

North: Marcie Haynes—Grandmother—who always found the courage to dream.

South: Dr. Martha Carmichael—Mentor and Counselor—who expresses the courage to see current reality with compassion.

East: Leif Diamant—Friend and Advisor—who demonstrates the courage to confront what most of us avoid.

West: Bob Staub—Father, Leader, Patriot—who learned and came to express the courage to be confronted by life.

Up: Dr. Richard Moss—Mentor and Teacher—who walks forward with a resounding "yes" to the acts of courage to learn and grow.

Down: Jeanie Haynes Staub—Mother and Teacher—who expresses the courage to be vulnerable and to love.

Within: Dr. Christine von Clemm Staub—Wife, Healer, Mother of My Children—who always expresses the courage to act, regardless of self-doubts or opposition from the powers that be.

Bringing Spirit to All You Do:
Living and Leading Wholeheartedly

"Be the change you want to see in the world."
                                                    - Mahatma Gandhi

For many years now, I have been writing, talking, coaching and consulting on the need for organizations, communities, families and individuals to develop the courage to live and lead more wholeheartedly. That theme has taken on an increased urgency since the horrific events of September 11, 2001 in the United States. We will need more, not less courage as well as more heartfelt leadership as we move forward.

Since the events of that day of violence and senseless destruction, most of us have moved along a spectrum of shock and disbelief into anger, anguish and into determination and hope. Since September 11th, any suffering in the world, even in faraway Afghanistan, can be seen as the breeding ground for hatred, threatening all of us, no matter where we live. We are challenged to find the courage to not only see the starkness of current reality, but also to have the courage to dream of a better world, and to act on that dream. As Robert Kennedy so eloquently expressed it, "Most see the world as it is and ask why. I see what could be and ask, 'Why not?'"

A poll taken since the violence of September 11th says that one out of every four workers is not able to focus on work due to anxiety. For them, the mundane tasks of work seem pointless and there is a state of fear while waiting for the "other shoe to drop." Yet, this anxiety can be used to focus us on how to live more courageously and wholeheartedly. Indeed, there is a collective hunger for something more meaningful than simply going to work to do a job and getting a paycheck, of being too intensely focused on getting and having.

Our world is rapidly changing its contours and characteristics as we wrestle with the challenges of globalization, the collapse of illusions of safety, and the shrinking of timelines due to living and working at the accelerated pace. We risk being emotionally and psychologically overwhelmed in the process, diminishing our effectiveness, our capacity to love wholly and to live fully. There is the very real danger of losing our resiliency and capacity to bounce back when we encounter great difficulty or have a head on collision with the unexpected..

Most of us are struggling with how to cope amidst rapid change, uncertainty, threats of violence and fear. If we are to successfully deal with the fear both within and around us, we will need to strengthen our courage muscle. Since the word courage is derived from the Latin for "heart" this means finding the means to deepen our connection with our own heart as well as with the hearts of those around us. We need to find the courage to live more wholeheartedly. This means developing our ability to access and use all seven of the acts of courage outlined in this book.

How can you bring a deeper sense of meaning and value to all of your life, your family, community, workplace, nation and world? How can you cultivate the courage to "Be" the difference? This slim book offers more than just inspiring stories and examples. It also provides answers and clear practices that can help you to live more courageously, while developing personal mastery and leadership qualities through small, daily acts of courage.

In truth, we all need to learn faster, work more innovatively, confront more honestly and respectfully, welcome confrontation, and be able to sustain and renew ourselves. Yet it is impossible to do so if we fail to invite and make room for a deeper sense of meaning, for more heart in all aspects of our lives.

"The Seven Acts of Courage" provides illuminating stories on the efficacy of courage in arenas ranging from the deeply personal, to the family, to organizations and society. It also offers clear, practical guidelines and exercises to help you develop your personal courage quotient. Take it to heart and you will find yourself living and leading more wholeheartedly. Prepare to be the change you wish to see in the world.

TABLE OF CONTENTS

Sing a song of glory, and you'll be that glory;
Naught are you but song, and as you sing you are.

You thought you were the teacher,
and find you are the taught;
You thought you were the seeker,
and find you are the sought.

Sing a song of glory, and you'll be that glory;
Naught are you but song, and as you sing, you are.

—Sufi Chant

INTRODUCTION

THE 7 ACTS OF COURAGE

I have a daring proposition for you: What you seek is also seeking you. Your life really matters. Who you are and what you are is precious and priceless, and you offer the world gifts it has never had before. You have within you vast potential and unique talents that yearn for expression, and for which the world around you hungers. You also have great power to exert. For example, whenever you change, the world around you also changes. You make a difference by realizing that you are the difference, and that you are needed. This realization places you on the pathway not only to giving the world what it needs, but to fulfilling your greatest dreams. You can make that difference—and your life—a powerful and positive force—but to walk this pathway and persist in it requires courage.

Any time we go after what we most want, or pursue something of importance, courage is required. It takes courage to step out of queue and pursue a dream, or to reach for your heart's desire. It means taking risks. It means letting go of the status quo and striving to create something that different parts of your psyche may doubt. It means facing hardship, ridicule, embarrassment, possibly failure, and, worst of all, your own internal criticism.

Courage is required because to live from the authentic center of who you are, and to pursue or protect what is most precious to you, is not easy in our society. Many naysayers, well-meaning colleagues, and friends, as well as the fearful inner voices within us, try to keep us in line. We are challenged to keep quiet, to conform, to step back into preassigned roles and ways of behaving. We are assailed by inner doubts and fears, sometimes by threats, but most often by misunderstanding and puzzlement, or by the not-so-subtle judgments of those who don't understand what we are doing, or who may be threatened by our increasing authenticity.

In the past 30 years I have had the privilege of working as a consultant with many "successful" executives and business owners as well as their families. What I have seen has been both inspiring and heart-breaking. These people have accomplished much to be proud of, but many suffer from constricting belief systems, overworked bodies and minds, neglected families, aching hearts, and spiritual hunger. Many are living as if their lives didn't matter.

I also have had the privilege of working with less "successful" members of our society: handicapped children, underprivileged families, financially strapped workers, and people on welfare. The sacrifice and personal triumph they often demonstrate is encouraging, yet the same pain can also be seen in their lives. These two diverse groups feel the same yearnings for a more vital experience of being alive, of feeling valued, and of feeling they make a difference.

I believe most of us are simply overwhelmed by change and by the incessant demands of the workplace, our families, and the society around us. Our senses are constantly assaulted as multiple entities jockey for our attention, time, and commitment. It becomes difficult to navigate the encroaching demands of each day and keep a firm grasp on our souls—remembering to nurture and nourish the core of who we are. We are drawn to the periphery of who we are, and we live from that edge, rather than the center. In the process, we lose our way. We lose touch with the vital center of our souls. As one executive put it, "I feel as if I have no self. All I do is struggle to meet the needs of my boss, the workplace, my children, and my aging parents. There's nothing left for me, or of me, by the time I fall into bed."

But there is a better way to live, a pathway to the center of your heart and of your life. It is not a long pathway. In fact, what you most desire is very close, but it may be difficult to take the steps to get there. To find the pathway and walk it requires daily acts of courage.

The Path of Heart

What, then, is "courage"? Where does it come from? How can you cultivate it and bring it into your personal and professional life?

The word "courage" comes from the French word "*coeur*," which means "heart." To practice courage, then, is to exercise acts of "heart." Courage comes from the heart and must return to it consistently for guidance and renewal. Courage is to remember the essential truths confirmed by the heart: that your life is precious, that you matter, and that you have wonderful gifts the world needs.

Courage is not to be found in one great heroic act, but in day-to-day actions that spring from the heart, and from your willingness to take the path of heart. To "take heart" is literally to call forth your deepest aspirations, to act based on what you believe is right, and to persist in the face of fear and in spite of the intimidation you may receive from others or feel inside yourself.

To own and direct your own life in all its dimensions requires the conscious and intelligent exercise of courage. This means demonstrating heart. Even more significant, "taking heart" often inspires and taps the motivation in others, who then follow your initiative. Thus, you become a leader to those around you, including your family, friends, and co-workers, as they become aware of your vision and integrity as you engage daily acts of courage.

Even if you do not see yourself as a leader, the presence of courage (or the lack of it) in your life makes a great difference in how you experience yourself and how you move through the day. For example, if we lack the courage to hear how we may have hurt someone we love, we do not listen to what they say; we damage their trust, their love, and thus the relationship. Or, if we lack the courage to tell the truth about what we feel or think, we do not express ourselves, and we end up feeling alienated or diminished. If we lack the courage to pursue our dreams, we end up with lower self-respect and a gnawing sense of inadequacy. If we lack the courage to reach out for the relationships we most desire, we end up with remorse and regret.

I am convinced that courage is desperately needed if we are to live lives of purpose, meaning, love, and fulfillment. Courage today is in short supply. The failure to find courage has led to an increasingly fragmented society filled with divisive personal and institutional agendas. Our political leaders, for the most part, demonstrate a penchant for expediency and the "quick fix," lacking the courage to tell the truth to the electorate. Many industrial leaders have also failed to demonstrate courage, seeking the lowest common denominator and the easiest answers when faced with the toughest questions and challenges in our rapidly evolving "information revolution." Candor and facing tough choices require courage, and courage could make great leaders of these same people if they, if we, could exercise it.

As a society we lack courage to face the truth about how we have been living and the decisions we have been making or avoiding. It is time to wake up and face the current realities of our age. We must somehow find within ourselves the heart to open our eyes and look beyond our expectations, hopes, fears, and past beliefs if we are to gaze unflinchingly upon what stands before us and what we must do.

The 7 Acts

What if the deepest part of your heart could find a more fulfilling and loving connection with life? What if you could live your life with greater awareness of how precious, valuable, and important life is? What if you could direct your life from the center of who you are, toward the realization of all you can do and all you can be?

Through the exercise and cultivation of seven acts of courage, you can start living your life today as if all aspects of who you are really mattered—creating a deeper, richer connection to your heart and to the hearts of those around you day by day. Each day then contributes to a deeper and more satisfying sense of purpose, vitality, and aliveness. Each day you grow stronger in your capacity to exercise love, enjoyment, and power in your life.

I have identified seven distinct acts of courage needed to create the lives we most desire and to live our lives from that place of greater authenticity. These acts encompass the whole of who we are and who we can be. The seven acts of courage are:

1. The courage to dream and put forth that dream.
2. The courage to see current reality.
3. The courage to confront.
4. The courage to be confronted.
5. The courage to learn and grow.
6. The courage to be vulnerable, to love.
7. The courage to act.

These acts of courage work on different aspects of our psychological being. They strengthen and refine the connections between our internal world and the external world. These acts help us develop increasing levels of personal power, efficacy, and ability. Each one strengthens our capacity to relate meaningfully to every moment while building our ability to create more effective and loving relationships with others. The acts of courage connect us to our higher selves, to the dimension of the spirit, and open us up to more constant communion with God.

You don't need, at this point, proficiency in all of the acts to achieve success or create a more joyful life. Simply learning which act to call forth, and practicing that act, allows you to function at higher levels anywhere, with anyone, and at any time. In fact, try to build your courage quotient one act at a time. Each time you act with courage, even if it's only a small act, you build capacity for your next, perhaps larger, act of courage and expand the power and authenticity of your self-expression.

Use this list to help you become more powerful and effective. For example, select the acts of courage you have no difficulty with, the ones you practice easily and often. These are strengths you can build from. Then consider the acts of courage you don't often practice, that you avoid or simply haven't worked on. Begin today to consciously cultivate your courage quotient by practicing these underused acts. By focusing on these unpracticed acts, and by using the guidelines in the following chapters, you can significantly increase your personal power, effectiveness, and satisfaction in life.

Ask yourself, which act of courage do you most need to practice on a day-by-day basis? What situations are you currently facing that could be transformed by acting with courage? What have you been avoiding that you most need to face? Which act of courage will be most helpful in dealing with it? The seven acts of courage can help you diagnose and prescribe—for individuals, couples, leaders, teams, and organizations—a new framework for dialogue, understanding, and mutual focus.

Why are there seven acts? Why not just two, or three? Why not twelve? Seven acts are required because it takes that many to capture the fullness, range, and depth of the courageous actions required for a "wholehearted" life. In fact, we are touched by the number seven in our lives and psyches every day: There are seven days in each week. The number seven, historically, has been a symbol of wholeness; and, religiously, since ancient times it has been a sacred number. We are impacted by seven-year cycles. Our bodies regenerate themselves every seven years. There are seven major directions: north, south, east, west, up, down, and within. Seven, then, signifies completion. Certainly we can think of other acts of courage by narrowing and focusing, or by using different words to describe similar things. But I feel the seven acts described in this book encompass the courage that leads to the completion of the soul.

The Law of Correspondence

As you build courage, and as you prepare to take the next steps in going after what you really want in life, you can apply what I call the "Law of Correspondence." This law says that an image or metaphor for your goal can be used in a literal sense to prepare you for a larger action. The image "corresponds" with the action you need to take. So, by beginning with small actions that correspond to your goal, you are prepared to take much larger steps. In fact, these smaller, "practice" acts of courage often move you further down the path toward your heart's desire than if you had taken larger steps without being prepared.

Let me illustrate from my own experience. Earlier in my career I was working for a thriving consulting company. I had status, a decent salary and benefits, and appreciative clients. I also had a wife, a six-month-old baby boy, and a mortgage. Yet, in my heart, I knew I wanted to create my own organization. I believed there was a better way to serve clients like mine, and I wanted to see what I was capable of creating. But the thought of founding and growing a company both excited and terrified me. I knew what I wanted to do and saw how it might be done, but I was frozen with fear. I needed to call forth and practice the seventh act of courage: the courage to act.

For about six months I thought through all the logistics of launching a new business, writing a plan and working out a potential strategy. I acted on the first act: the courage to dream and put forth that dream. My wife encouraged me to go for it and helped me figure out how we could manage with virtually no money coming in. I applied the second act: the courage to see current reality. The next step was the leap.

And that's exactly what it felt like. It was like I was standing at the edge of a cliff, looking across a deep chasm toward a beautiful meadow, with no idea of how to reach it. I felt paralyzed by the fear of taking that leap, of risking the security I had for the promise of what I thought I could create. And there I sat, in doubt, fear, and indecision, for about four months.

I needed more courage than I currently possessed, and the internal critic within me was working overtime. After all, I had been encouraging executives to exercise more courage, but when I was faced with taking my own leap to create what I deeply desired, I was holding back. Then the breakthrough came. I discovered the law of correspondence—that a corresponding image or metaphor can be used literally to prepare you for action. For me, the image was "taking a leap."

Since I was feeling the sensation of taking a leap at a physical level, I began to play with that image. It may sound silly, but I started practicing my leaping abilities. I drew lines in the dirt and practiced the broad jump. I tried to stretch a little further each time, feeling the sensation of my muscles bunching beneath me and my body hurtling through space.

One afternoon during this time, my wife Tina and I were walking through the woods along a stream behind our house. We came to a point where the opposite bank of the stream rose about fifteen feet above where we were standing. In the middle of the stream was a long branch that had fallen, its upper end resting on the opposite bank at a 45-degree angle. Suddenly, I was struck by inspiration. I would leap to the branch, which was only a few feet from where we were, and walk up the branch to the bank on the other side. This would be a test of my readiness to "leap" and then navigate the after-effects of the leap.

Could I catch my balance on the branch without falling into the water? Could I walk up the steep slope to the opposite bank? I told Tina what I was thinking, and she laughed, telling me I was crazy. Yet I knew, at an intuitive level, that this was preparation for the even larger "leap" I would be making.

I took off my coat. Tina was now trying to talk some sense into me as she realized I was serious. I rocked back and forth and then sprang forward, landing with both feet on the branch and catching my balance as I wavered for a moment between falling forward or backward. After I found my balance, I stood triumphantly upon the branch and looked over to Tina. She looked a little shocked, but then smiled at me. I turned my attention to the branch, quickly walked up, and stepped onto the bank above. Looking down at Tina on the opposite bank, I bowed and she laughed, offering her congratulations. I walked down the stream to a lower point and walked across some rocks, tracing my way back to Tina.

"I'm going to try that again, to show myself it wasn't a fluke," I explained. Tina now offered some encouragement, sensing something important was happening inside of me. Again I leaped, repeating my success. As I landed the second time, I felt elated. All my fears began to fall away. I walked up the branch again and, at the top, felt a tremendous sense of freedom. I repeated the thing a third time, but it was anticlimactic by then. I knew I was ready to leave my current job and "leap" to the new venture. I also knew I could make the leap, and, come what may, my family and I would be okay.

As we walked away, I turned to Tina and said, "I am ready to do it. Regardless of whether I succeed or fail, I want to be able to tell our son when he's older that I had the courage to take the leap and go after what I really wanted. That's part of the legacy I want to leave him, that he can go after his heart's desire without fearing failure."

If there is something you would like to do, but your fear or self-doubts hold you back, find an image or metaphor that reflects what you want to do. Play with the image, find a way to physically embody it and to practice doing what you want at a symbolic level. For me it was "taking a leap." For you, it might be "stepping out," "revealing yourself," "hanging out a shingle," "turning off" old behaviors, or "embracing" a new way of being. Whatever the image, use it as a means of exercising and developing your courage, for preparing yourself for the larger act of courage to create what you most deeply desire.

The law of correspondence says you don't need to have all the courage right now. Instead, you can develop the courage you need over a period of days, or even months, as you safely practice with a living image or metaphor of the action you want to take. You can develop your courage on a daily basis in this way.

A wealthy, high-powered executive I worked with realized one day that he had been so busy building his career and developing his company he had become a stranger to his family. He had lost his center, working eighty hours per week. His health and his heart were damaged. He wanted to develop a more intimate and loving relationship with his eleven-year-old son, especially since his wife had just left him and he only had visitation rights a few times a week.

"It's too late for my marriage, but I hope it's not too late for my son and me," he said. Yet, when he was with his son, he found himself constricted, anxious, uncomfortable, and awkward. He was afraid to take the relationship to a deeper level, and he felt pained to discover that he didn't know how to talk to his son in a meaningful way. His son had become a stranger to him—and an angry, demanding, and difficult stranger at that.

I asked him to find an image that would correspond with what he wanted to create with his son. He struggled with this for a few minutes and then said, "Look, all I want is to feel that my son and I are walking together, in synch, as we discover some exciting adventures." I encouraged him to take that image of walking together as the key to creating a new relationship with his son.

Soon they began to take walks along the old canals in town, simply discovering the old waterways. As they walked, the father not only found physical relaxation, but he soon found himself tentatively and awkwardly moving into emotional discovery and revelation. He shared his regrets with his son about what he had missed out on with the family. By the fifth walk, his son began to soften his angry tone and to share, with tears, how much he had missed him. The boy also began to talk about himself, and what a stupid, no-good person he thought he was. His father, appalled at the boy's self-image, shared how proud he was of his son and how much he loved him. The boy then told his father how he thought something must be wrong with him since his father never spent any time with him. Then both father and son wept together.

Over the next four months, the image of walking together helped both the father and son grow in their capacity for greater acts of courage, allowing them to reveal deeper emotions to each other and discover new dimensions of themselves in the process. During their many walking adventures, the father developed the courage to be vulnerable, and found greater intimacy with himself and his son as a result. The boy also developed the courage to confront and to be confronted, and was able to share his self-doubts with a loving and attentive father who could help. As the two began to walk toward each other, they not only were able to exercise and strengthen their relationship, they began to heal their respective "heart" conditions as well.

Each chapter in this book focuses on one act of courage, helping you understand how the different acts work on various parts of your soul and spirit. The chapters will help you develop your capacity to access and exercise the acts of courage as you need them. At the end of each chapter is a summary of the major points, along with exercises designed to make the concepts come alive in your life. Although you may already be practiced in some of the acts of courage, the exercises will help you attend to and strengthen them on a more conscious level. Keep in mind: The acts you do not yet practice are the ones that hold the keys to unlocking your potential and living your life more joyfully and wholeheartedly.

SUMMARY AND EXERCISES:

Using the Law of Correspondence

First: Resolve today to begin to live your life in a wholehearted way, knowing that each act of courage really matters. Begin by thinking about what is most important to you. Write down your answers to the following seven questions:

1. What do you most deeply desire?
2. What is most precious in your life?
3. What forms the center of your life experience?
4. If you could live and experience your life as you truly want, what would you do differently? How would you feel?
5. What are the deepest guiding values and principles by which you seek to live?
6. If you could change your life for the better, so that you were living from what is deepest and best in you, what would you change?
7. What would that change do for you in terms of living from your heart?

Second: Resolve to begin to find and create the courage to live from your center, honoring the depth and richness of your heart. Look for opportunities to exercise "daily acts of courage."

• Start by asking yourself what you would like to do, but are afraid to try.

• Find a corresponding image or metaphor that captures the essence of what you want to do. Some examples include: "taking a leap," "walking in harmony," "spending time on discovery and exploration," "embracing something new," "hunkering down and enduring," "turning over a new leaf," and "dancing to a new tune." Find an image that speaks to your heart.

• Once you have found a corresponding image or symbol, create a means for engaging the image in a daily activity. For example, if you have chosen the image of "dancing to a new tune," find a new song or form of music you have never danced to, and then dance to it. Dance privately at first, and then look for opportunities to dance with others. The act of dancing to a new tune will help you begin the process of learning something new, and help you make the larger change you hope to make. When you risk the embarrassment of not getting the steps right with the new tune, you are exercising courage and preparing yourself for the larger act of courage that will follow. In the meantime, you are taking steps toward greater courage and capacity in a non-threatening manner.

THE FIRST ACT

THE COURAGE TO DREAM AND PUT FORTH THAT DREAM

"Sing a song of glory . . ."

The courage to dream and put forth your dream is essential if you are to claim the power to create your life and bring out the best in yourself and others. It is the first act of courage because it provides a context for all the other acts. It allows you to orient yourself at any time and in any place, based on a consistent vision that forms the inner core of your amazing strength. This act allows you to pursue what you most desire, pulling you toward a more powerful sense of self and self-worth.

This act of courage requires simply that you claim all you aspire to be. What is your dream, your deepest desire? What do you hold most dear? What would you bring to life if you could? What is the "song of glory" you wish to sing?

What does it mean to "sing a song of glory"? I have an idea: Remember, if you can, Martin Luther King, Jr.'s "I Have a Dream" speech. Dr. King developed and refined his dream over many years and gave voice to his "song of glory," his dream of a nation undivided by prejudice and hatred. Many listened to his song and took courageous steps toward greater racial equality and harmony as a result. But the song is not finished and did not die with him. The song lives on, touching and inspiring others with its power and affirmation, and people continue to sing that song of freedom and equality. His courage to dream and put forth that dream has been a great gift for us all.

What Is Your Song?

Perhaps your "song of glory" is to be a loving parent, ensuring that your children grow up healthy and whole, confident in their self-worth, and knowing how much they are loved. Or maybe it is to create a new business, or a product or service, providing meaningful employment for others. Or it may be to write a book, direct a film, or teach a course, reaching out to touch the hearts and minds of many. Whatever your "song of glory" is, you must first find the courage to articulate the lyrics and then to "sing the song."

This song comes from deep within your heart. To sing it requires your full capacity to tap the tremendous power of imagination, create images that capture your deepest longing, and then communicate those images. You can tap into and formulate images that reflect your highest aspirations and greatest desires, all coming together in an integrated rhythm that you can move to, and from which you can create. This is the beat of your song.

To identify your song and then sing it requires the courage to appear naive, to challenge your self-limiting beliefs, to defy your circumstances, and to face the judgments, criticisms, and cynicisms of others. If you do not cultivate this primary act of courage, you risk missing out. You may leave your greatest gifts and talents undeveloped that could otherwise enrich and edify others. You will lack orientation, the context for guiding and directing your actions and the actions of those around you. You will wonder why life seems dull and meaningless. In fact, you may miss out on singing the very song you came here to sing. Instead, you could be left standing silent before the vast mystery of life, or merely playing your part in the cacophony of general noise around you. You leave your life in the hands of chance and the decisions of others.

On the other hand, to practice the courage to dream and put forth your dream is to say:

> *When it's over, I want to say: All my life*
> *I was a bride married to amazement.*
>
> *I was the bridegroom, taking the world into my arms.*
> *When it's over, I don't want to wonder*
>
> *If I have made of my life something particular and real.*
> *I don't want to find myself sighing and frightened, or*
> *full of argument.*
>
> *I don't want to end up simply*
> *having visited this world.*

—excerpt from Mary Oliver, "When Death Comes"

The courage to dream and put forth that dream requires that you formulate a vision for your life. You must craft your dream, refining it through each major challenge you face. Then, you must communicate your vision—whether in a relationship, a team, at work, or in the community—and engage others in its creation. As you live your dream, clarifying and articulating it as you go, you give voice to your own unique "song of glory."

Intention and Attention

This act of courage comes first since it sets the tone and direction, and establishes meaning, for the other six acts, providing a foundation for your life. It works at the soul level through two simple mechanisms: First, your dream or vision activates the power of intention— what you truly wish could be as a result of what you do or say. Second, putting forth your dream then activates, in your day-to-day behavior, the power of attention— what you focus on and what continually draws you toward the accomplishment of your intention.

Intention is the power of choosing an internal compass and reference point. It guides the way you live your life, and it defines, as you interact with people and situations, what you wish to create—not only in your life, but also in any project, work group, or enterprise in which you are involved. Intention is the creative purpose that informs and directs all you do, both in your personal life and in your career. It provides coherence, meaning, and purpose to all your activities. For example, if one part of your dream is to create a loving, nurturing relationship with your family, then your "intention" is to love and let yourself be loved, to nurture and be nurtured. This intention provides a context for all interactions with your family.

Richard Moss, author of *The Second Miracle*, uses the word "consecration" when asking people what they intend to do with their lives. By this, he means: What are you consecrating, making sacred, or giving your life over to? What is the aim of your life, and what drives you? Consecration is your deepest intention; it is the lodestar that provides orientation and direction.

Attention is the power of focusing your consciousness and life energy in the present. This power gives traction to your vision and supplies the means of manifesting what you intend. Using the example above, it is not enough simply to intend to love others and be loved by them. Intention is only the first step. The next step is to express that intention in your words and actions by paying attention to how you respond to family members and others. Attention means noticing what works, as well as what doesn't work and what gets in the way of creating what you intend.

Attention is the practice of being mindful, of noticing what is going on, while observing your behavior. Attention then provides clues to behaviors that are off purpose with what you intend and to which you are blind. It clarifies what works and what doesn't work for you in making your dreams reality.

Research conducted at Harvard University over the course of fifty years indicated that the university's most successful graduates each cultivated the practice of writing down their goals and then focusing on them. "Success," as measured by the study, did not occur so much as a result of intelligence quotients, class scores, or extracurricular activities, but it occurred most often for those who had learned to focus their attention by writing their goals.

The Courage to Put Forth Your Dream

When Tina and I became engaged, we sat down and wrote out our "dreams" for our marriage. Then we carefully questioned each other and made comments as we elaborated a vision statement. We defined and clarified what we wanted from ourselves, each other, and the union itself. This exercise formed both the individual and joint intentions for our lifelong commitment to each other. But, even though it took several days of soul-searching and conversation, that was the easy part. The second, and much harder, part was to remain conscious of, and attend to, the different ways our words and actions supported our intentions.

One evening, a few weeks after we had drafted our vision, we found ourselves arguing. She had called me "stupid" and then pretended nothing had happened. I became upset, provoked by all the self-doubt I carried, and by the hurt I felt. But, instead of sharing my pain, I became self-righteous and, in a lecturing tone, said, "I certainly don't call you names. It is unloving and not in keeping with our vision for this relationship for you to do so." But instead of seeing the error of her ways and apologizing, Tina simply withdrew and refused to talk with me. So, out of pain and fear, I upped the ante, saying, "Well, maybe we should simply forget the wedding!" Then I stormed off. She came after me with a vengeance, angry and hurt.

As I looked at her face I saw the effect of my words and actions, and I knew, with a pang, how much I had hurt her. I paid attention to her pain, and I remembered what I had intended to create in my relationship with her. I felt ashamed at what I had done. Then I apologized. "I blew it," I said. "You deserve much better than the way I've been acting. I'm sorry."

She took my hands and we looked at each other, seeing the pain and the longing we both carried—not the defensiveness and self-righteousness we had perfected in the years before we met. We restated our dreams and reminded each other of our intentions for our relationship. The pull of our dreams, our combined vision, was compelling. We then talked through our conflict, learning from each other and deepening our understandings about old wounds and defenses. And, because we had the courage to view our argument in the context of our collective vision, we arrived at a deeper level of intimacy.

It takes courage to admit to yourself the truth of what you want to be and wish to create. It often requires deep soul-searching, exploring the beliefs, fears, and judgments that block you from clearly formulating and articulating your dreams. It also takes courage to put your dreams forward, to remember them in the day-to-day struggles, to restate them and shift their context to a higher purpose. Often, it takes the courage to risk feeling embarrassed or awkward.

A highly successful senior executive in a *Fortune* 500 company had just been reprimanded by her boss. As she fumed about the encounter, she glared at me: "How dare they do this to me; I've done everything for them! Everything! I don't deserve this kind of treatment. It's the work of a disaffected few, poisoning the well. Well, I won't stand for it!"

She was beside herself with fury and rage. Yet I also saw, at a deeper level, that she was hurt and shocked by what had happened. As I listened to her pour out her anger and pain, I wondered how such a competent and committed executive could be so blindsided by her own staff, a staff she cared deeply about. As she calmed down a little, she stopped pacing and sat down. In a plaintive tone, with her head in her hands, she asked, "What did I do wrong?"

She continued, "My staff is afraid of me; they say I treat them with contempt!" She went on to explain how she had worked to make her staff successful, and how proud she was of their accomplishments—that is, until her boss came to her with the complaints.

She was a no-nonsense, results-focused manager. She drove herself and her people hard toward ambitious goals and high standards. Those who worked for her both respected and feared her. She was quick to criticize what she viewed as performance-endangering behaviors, and, because excellence was expected, it was never praised. She was passionate about success, but, as one team member put it, "It's like she's on a mission from God, but no one is clear about how we fit into that mission. Only one thing is clear: Nothing had better get in her way!"

As we talked, I discovered that this executive cared deeply about the success of each member of her team. I asked her to outline what her intentions had been, and then I asked if she had ever shared those intentions with her associates. She said she had always believed actions speak louder than words and that her team knew about her intentions. She explained that she really didn't like "touchy-feely" stuff and felt awkward about discussing anything other than quotas, tasks, and goals with her team. She held back praise because she felt embarrassed, and she didn't want to appear idealistic or naive by expressing an impossible-sounding vision. She was stunned and hurt to discover how her behavior created the opposite of what she intended.

This executive had gotten herself into trouble by not exercising the first act of courage. She had allowed her fear of being embarrassed to stop her, assuming the team would simply know her intentions and feelings. She had lacked the courage to articulate her dream, and so the team lacked context for her actions. Instead, she had left the team to fill in the blanks, which meant they would interpret her behavior from the perspective of their anxieties. They had not understood what she was striving for, or how they fit into her plans. The only organizing force for the team was her personality, the goals she set, and her corrective feedback to team members. She had failed to call forth their aspirations and provide a reason for them to take risks with her. And ultimately, the team saw no way to resolve team conflicts and problems.

Over the course of the next few hours, we discussed the team's perceptions and how those perceptions were created. We discussed her tactics as a manager and her conscious and unconscious behaviors in dealing with her team. Then we charted an intervention with her team to help her begin the change process. The executive and her team went on to create a shared vision and strategy for working together, and the team went on to become a powerhouse of excellence in the organization. Members of the team were sought out by other departments and teams because of their ability to articulate a dream and work together to achieve it.

The power of exercising the courage to dream, of actually singing your "song of glory," is awesome. It clarifies and defines your intentions. Then, it becomes the guiding star on which to focus your attention and the attention of others. It boldly expresses your heart's aim.

SUMMARY AND EXERCISES:

Developing the Courage to Dream and Put Forth That Dream

"Sing a song of glory . . ."

The courage to dream and put forth your dream is essential to creating and living your life with greater authenticity, effectiveness, and personal power. It forms the backbone of a consistent and loving sense of direction and orientation, allowing you to direct your attention in all that you do, so that you can manifest your intentions. It forms the creative center of a joyful and fulfilling life.

First: Unleash the power of conscious intention. Take time right now to reflect on where you want to go and what you wish to accomplish. What is the "dream" for your life? What do you intend to experience, create, do, be?

Exercise: Unleashing the Power of Imagery to Create Your Dream. Gather a stack of different magazines and newspapers and cut out the pictures that appeal to you or to which you are drawn. As you search for images, keep asking yourself: "What is the dream for my life? How would I like to experience and create my life?" After you have selected the images you like best, take a large piece of paper or cardboard (16" x 18" is a good size) and arrange the images into a collage. For added effect, you may also select things you can feel. Make it a collage of visual and kinesthetic images.

• List your goals and aspirations. What is the underlying theme running through your list? Summarize the theme in two sentences. Notice how you feel about the two sentences.

• Arrange the two sentences into a vision statement that speaks to your heart even more than to your head. Make sure it's what you really want, whether or not you believe you can make it happen. Make sure the statement captures how you would like to experience your life and relate to others, as well as what you would like to achieve. Notice the feelings your statement evokes.

• Read your vision statement out loud in front of a mirror, looking at your eyes as much as possible. Notice your feelings and observe any doubts. Believe in the importance of the vision, even if your mind says it can't be realized.

• Consciously choose your vision. Make the statement "I choose this vision. I choose to believe in it, in spite of any doubts."

• Find someone who cares about you and who you trust to share the vision statement with. Ask for his or her support.

Second: Unleash the power of conscious attention. Help make your dream a reality by focusing on it and by bringing the power of attention to bear on what you are doing, what is going on around you, and how your behaviors work to serve you or work against what you most aspire to do and be.

• Write your vision statement, your dream, on several 3" x 5" cards. Post the cards in highly visible places such as your refrigerator, car visor, bathroom mirror, desk, next to your computer screen, or on the inside of your planner; carry a copy in your pocket or purse, or use a copy as a bookmark.

• First thing in the morning, occasionally during the day, and the last thing at night, look at your vision statement and repeat it to yourself out loud. Remind yourself about what you most desire and about your aspirations.

• Find opportunities to talk about your vision and your commitment to it with people you trust and who care about you.

• Observe your interactions with others and notice what works to draw you closer to your vision, as well as what doesn't work; consider what you do, whether habitually or reactively, that may be working against the realization of your vision.

Third: Harness the synergy of intention and attention in all you do. Now that you have created and fine-tuned your dream, you must actively cultivate the courage to create secondary, or functional dreams in your major life activities. These secondary dreams serve to reinforce, and move you toward, the realization of your life vision. It is your "song of glory," and you are working to make it a living reality.

- List the major activities going on in your life at this moment. For example, one executive listed the following: parenting, leading a work team, heading up a major project, coaching his daughter's soccer team, dealing with a dying parent, and maintaining his marriage.

- For each of the activities, starting with the most significant, write out the outcome you wish to create, specify your intentions, and put them on paper. These form the secondary dreams or visions in your life that support your overall life vision.

- Condense these secondary statements into one or two sentences at most.

- Write out a brief statement about how all your secondary dreams reinforce and support your overall dream.

- Revise your statements based on what you see and feel. Make sure each of your dreams interlock in your mind and reinforce what you most deeply desire to experience and create in your life.

- Sit down with important people in your life and share your secondary vision for your interactions with them. Let them react. Ask them for their thoughts and feelings.

- Invite them to create with you a unified set of intentions, along with some guidelines on how to help each other focus attention on the realization of these goals.

THE SECOND ACT

THE COURAGE TO SEE CURRENT REALITY

". . . And you'll be that glory."

If the first act of courage, to dream and put forth that dream, is the foundation for creating your life in a meaningful and powerful way, then the second act, the courage to see current reality, is the ground upon which that foundation stands. It is the willingness to listen to and notice the current song of your life: How are you singing it and experiencing it? What results are you creating? What are you expressing? How are you feeling? What is working and not working? What have you made of your life so far?

It takes great courage to see current reality—and to see it clearly—without using the great defenses of the ego, such as pretense, excuse, denial, blame, or rationalization. Your current reality includes not only the things you are proud of, and all your accomplishments, it also includes the things of which you are ashamed, or that you would rather forget, or that you just won't see. It includes your defeats and losses. For most of us, it is easy to justify or deny our culpability in problematic relationships, troubled work environments, or disappointments in life. It is hard to see and own the places where our living experience is painful, constrained, or diminished. It is difficult to accept the criticisms of others. These painful experiences are the sum of our losses, disappointments, and self-doubts. They indicate where we have abandoned our power by giving in to fear or self-limiting beliefs.

Courage is required to look at current reality, especially the parts we don't wish to see and that we have skillfully avoided. When we do not take stock of present reality, we dupe ourselves and make it difficult, if not impossible, to correct behaviors that undermine our intentions.

Why is the courage to face current reality so essential? And, if it is so important, why is it number two on the list—why not make it number one?

It is essential to see and understand where you stand in the world, to observe what is working and not working in your life. If you do not know where you stand and how things really are in your life, you have no accurate reckoning, no basis for moving forward. You have no place from which to push, no ground to provide traction as you go about making your dream a reality. Yet, without the courage to dream and put forth that dream, you have nothing to move toward. Looking only at current reality leads to one of two dangerous reactions: If your current reality is comfortable, it leads to complacency; if it is painful or difficult, it leads to cynicism or despair.

In 1956, my father was assigned to command the U.S. Army base in Stiffkey, England. During the transfer of command, he was asked to sign a form certifying that all goods on the base were present and accounted for, and that he now accepted responsibility for them. This included all weapons, munitions, fuel, vehicles in the motor pool, as well as products in the Base Exchange store. By signing the form, he would be certifying that he was accepting accountability for all the goods listed and that they were, in fact, present at the time of signature.

Usually, in such transfers, the incoming commander would conduct a simple walk-through inspection and then verify with the previous commander that all was in order. But Dad, a captain taking charge of his first base, was nervous. He also had a penchant for detail. So, rather than a walk-through inspection, he undertook an extensive personal inspection of every major item on the inventory list to satisfy himself that all was in order. The departing base commander, a major, could not leave nor relinquish command until the inspection was completed and the form was signed. Since he outranked my father, he ordered him to cease the inspection and sign the form. Dad respectfully declined. The major became angry, accusing him of holding up his departure, but my father resisted the pressure until he could complete his inspection.

At the end of the inspection, my father told the major he could not sign the form since some significant items were missing from the inventory. The major then called the commanding general and complained that this insubordinate young officer was holding up his departure and calling him a liar—after all, the major had already told my father all the goods were on the base.

Dad was in agony about what to do; he wanted desperately to take over the base, and did not want to rock the boat. He just wanted to sign the form and get it over with, but he could not do so in good conscience. Seeing no other alternative, he began a recount.

At this point, the commanding general paid my father a visit and inquired "what in the hell" he was doing, delaying the major's departure and holding up the administration of the entire base. My father explained that he simply couldn't account for over a quarter million dollars' worth of inventory which the manifest said should be on the base. At this, the general lost his temper and called my father some names that would probably scorch this page if I were to repeat them. Then he ordered my father to sign the form and be done with it.

My father, trying to stop the trembling in his hands and legs, took the pen from the general. He faced, in that moment, two dreadful options: He could sign the form—after all, the goods were probably on the base somewhere; someone had probably just messed up the inventory. Things like this were known to happen all the time, and maybe he was being too rigid. Besides, he now faced a direct order. Or, he could follow his instincts and risk severe reprimand. His career could go up in flames, and he had a wife and three young children to support.

He leaned forward to sign the paper, feeling relieved but, at the same time, cowardly. He put the pen to the line for his signature and then paused. The pause lengthened. The general cleared his throat and said, "Captain, just sign the damned thing. Do it now!"

Then my father laid the pen down, stood at attention, and said, "Sir, I cannot sign it." Though he felt terrified, he also felt he had just won a major victory.

The general glared at him and asked, "Captain, are you refusing to obey a direct order? Think about your career; it's hanging in the balance."

My father replied, "General, I respectfully refuse to obey an order which requires that I falsify a report to the Army. You may very well wreck my career for this, but sir, you have no right to order me to lie or misrepresent the truth. I am liable for what I sign, and if I sign this, I am stating that the manifest is correct and that all the items are on the base. Sir, more than a quarter-million dollars of goods cannot be accounted for. They are missing. I will not lie, nor will I sign for what is not there." My father was terrified by what he had said, but he clearly saw current reality. In spite of his fear and his desires to please his superior officers, he stood by what he knew in that moment to be correct.

After a long pause, the general signed the form in his own name, saying, "Captain, I regret you have made this choice. You will live to regret defying me." Then he saluted my father and said, "Assume command of the base. The major is relieved." Dad returned the salute and left the room on rubbery legs.

Later, my father found out there had been an ongoing theft ring operating at the base, and that the major and the general had been colluding in the operation. Not only had my father made the ethical choice, but he also had been wise. His ability to see current reality not only protected him in that instance, it ultimately furthered his career.

To see the reality in front of you, in spite of the reality everyone wants you to see, is a daunting task. We face great pressure to conform to established norms. Often, we are ridiculed, threatened, shamed, or punished for defying conventional viewpoints. It takes great courage to step back and honestly assess the current reality. For want of doing so, many people in all walks of life have failed themselves and their enterprises. They have failed, their businesses have suffered, many families have been adversely impacted, and they, themselves, have been replaced.

Once, I was called in to consult with a manufacturing company. The president seemed open and eager to make his organization function at a higher level. I asked him to tell me about the company's business plan and strategy. He had a clear vision of what the organization needed to do and a well-thought-out plan. He had acted on the first act of courage, daring to dream and to put forth the dream in a strategic plan.

Next, we assessed the company's current reality. When I asked about how the company functioned, especially at the senior management level, he acknowledged a few problems, but nothing serious. He explained that he empowered his associates, letting them manage themselves. He also mentioned that the company was owned by two brothers who made their fortunes by buying up, leveraging, and growing inexpensive companies. The president reported to them quarterly, but the brothers had left him virtually alone to manage the business. "They are strictly hands off," he said.

Then I interviewed each of the president's direct reports on the executive team. Each one described an organization with great strengths, but that currently faced a severe crisis. The senior executives, all competent and bright individually, saw themselves as a dysfunctional team. The company's margins had begun to erode. Manufacturing problems were cropping up, and quality was now an issue. Each described the conflicts faced by management, but the president seemed unwilling or unable to help them function more effectively.

The executive team met weekly to discuss operations. The meetings would start at 8:00 in the morning and often ran until 8:00 at night. They frequently involved open shouting matches and long, drawn-out arguments. At the end of the meetings, the group typically broke up with no clear agreements or action plans. Everyone hated the meetings. The consensus was that during each twelve-hour session the team only accomplished about 45 minutes of real work.

When I next met with the president, I asked him what he expected to hear about the company's strengths and weaknesses. He accurately described the strengths, but he struggled a bit with the weaknesses. He had a clear view of the organization's challenges, but he was vague about the executive team's problems and showed little insight into his own weaknesses. I asked some probing questions, but he was unable to articulate anything else.

I asked the president if he was open to hearing some unpleasant information from his team, which, if he failed to address, would impair his progress toward making the organization more productive. His smile never wavered, and he said, "I've never been afraid to hear the truth, even when it's only the opinions of others."

At that moment, a little red light went off in my head about his readiness for the information. Since I felt he might not be ready to handle the team's feedback, we discussed the importance of perception and how it governs human behavior. Then I presented my summary.

The company faced three major challenges. I explained, "The first challenge involves the satisfaction of your key customers." He nodded his head in agreement. "The second challenge has to do with your direct reports and their collective dysfunction as a team."

He stopped smiling and remarked, "I think 'dysfunction' is too strong a word. I believe they're a good team; they just need a little fine-tuning."

Gently, I responded, "I understand you are proud of their abilities and that you see them as a team. But they do not see themselves as a team. They want to become a functional team, but they do not currently feel that they are one." He took out his pen and wrote a few lines on his notepad. Then he looked up, nodded, and asked, "Okay, what's the third challenge?"

I knew the president would have the most difficulty with the third point, but I knew he needed to hear it. "The third challenge involves your leadership and how to make it more powerful and effective." I elaborated, "Your direct reports appreciate your delegating to them, your belief in empowerment, and your patience in letting them work things out on their own. You are also an encouraging coach. But that is also the challenge you face in leading the team. Since the team is not operating well, they need you to step out of the coaching role and become a director, a leader. At the moment, your coaching style is working against the needs of the team; right now they need a leader."

The president put down his pen and looked out the window. "Thank you for your report. I'll think it over and give you a call." I tried to catch his eye but he refused to look at me.

"Sir," I said, "I would like to give you more substance and help you think through the best course of action."

But he was quite adamant about the session being finished. He stood up and extended his hand. I knew, with a sinking sensation, he was in deep denial. He wasn't going to look at current reality for his team or himself.

I took his hand and said, "Thank you for your time. Please consider what I've said. I know from experience that the owners you mentioned will not stay 'hands off' if the executive team continues to function as it has been and you do not address the challenges." Without a word, he sat down, picked up the phone, and dialed, dismissing me completely.

Nine months later I was informed that the owners had fired the president and all but one of the senior executives. The president had failed to see current reality. He failed himself, his "team," the owners, and the whole company. Instead of dealing with the reality his team faced, he acted according to what was most habitual and comfortable, crashing both his career and the business into the hard reality.

Why do so many intelligent people miss the obvious, focusing on what they wish to be true versus what is currently true and staring them in the face? The answer lies in how our minds distort reality to protect us from doubts or to protect our cherished assumptions and beliefs. For many of us, we simply do not wish to see something that indicates we might have to change our lives and our ways of doing things. Current reality can be inconvenient and downright unpleasant. It often challenges conventional wisdom. Courageously facing current reality means we may upset people who are unwilling to see it, and they will, in turn, pressure us to back down or subscribe to their viewpoint.

In the short term, not looking at current reality—whether in a relationship, your career, your business, or your own life—may protect you from pain. But, in the long term, if you do not cultivate the courage to see current reality, you set yourself up for much greater pain and failure.

We all have powerful psychological defenses we use to blind ourselves from seeing the current reality. It takes courage to challenge these defenses and see beyond them. They include:

- Denial
- Repression
- Projection and Distortion
- Rationalization

Denial

"Denial" is refusing to see what is in front of us. When faced with information that contradicts our view of reality, we refuse to acknowledge it. Sometimes, we do not even notice it is there at all. We are blinded by our prevailing mind-set and viewpoints. We do not allow ourselves to entertain or recognize any other perspective or alternative.

As in the case of the president with whom I consulted, denial makes unpleasant "facts" simply disappear. This is the "see no evil" monkey, with its hands clamped firmly over its eyes, blocking any viewpoints that may threaten or challenge current behaviors.

Denial, carried too far, destroys careers, relationships, even your health. We can easily recognize when someone close to us is refusing to see current reality. But the challenge is to recognize when we are doing the same. It takes courage to see past denial because it means we will have to change something in our lives or in the way we think.

Repression

"Repression" is a psychological defense that we use to block out and "forget" painful experiences. The event is so painful that we block out the memory of it and forget about it. However, repression of painful memories also means we block out the lessons we might learn from those experiences. Repression limits our ability to see reality, especially when it resembles the painful experiences we have repressed. We push the memory out of our minds to avoid pain and preserve the status quo. It takes courage, then, to see beyond repression because it means we will have to deal with whatever pain may still be there.

A young mother of two sought my help years ago when I had a clinical practice. She suffered from severe panic attacks, involving heart palpitations, nausea, and vertigo, and was convinced she was going to die. She had been hospitalized five times. The attacks had become so bad that she refused to go anywhere unless her mother could take her.

Over the course of six sessions she made some progress using various techniques to control panic attacks: breathing from her diaphragm, focusing her internal self-talk, using mental rehearsal, and learning various calming techniques. But the real breakthrough came when she worked up the courage to stop repressing her anger and frustration with her husband. She had been taught "good girls" don't get angry, so she would conceal her feelings from her family. But, when she could claim her anger and speak out for what she really wanted and needed, her anxiety completely disappeared. She became a powerhouse in her family and community. Her husband was delighted with the change, only now she was more challenging and demanding of him!

Projection and Distortion

Projection and distortion are defensive tools that allow us to shape and re-interpret the reality in front of us. It is hearing and seeing what we believe to be true, regardless of the reality we face. In a literal sense, we do not see what is in front of us, but we distort what is there and see, instead, a projected image or preconceived idea. We see our fears, doubts, wishes, hopes, expectations, beliefs, and ideals instead of what is really there. We distort what is "so" to fit our preconceived beliefs, prejudices, and feelings.

A common occurrence of projection is when we meet someone and immediately like or dislike them. Something about the person reminds us of someone else. We "project" onto them that same internal image and react accordingly.

When I first met my partner, Kirtland Peterson, we were working in another consulting firm. I immediately didn't like him. I saw him as arrogant, cold, and judgmental. But, understanding something of projection, I was suspicious of my first impression and made an effort to work with him and get to know him. I found him to be humane, sensitive, and delightful. Later, after our friendship had grown, I shared with him my first impressions. He laughed and told me he had felt the same way about me at first.

It takes courage to withdraw our projections, to check them and challenge them. They "feel" right and are largely unconscious, automatic responses. But, to live our lives as if they really mattered, to create joy, love, and long-term success, we must find the courage to challenge these automatic patterns within us. We must review our version of reality and see the truth.

Rationalization

Rationalization is the champion of psychological defenses, the most common and heavily favored. It is the defense used by everyone perhaps several times a day. Rationalization is explaining away any evidence that doesn't fit our viewpoint or self-definition. It is talking ourselves out of having to deal with unpleasant realities or having to face some painful issue. It is also a way of justifying something we want to do but know is "wrong."

For example, some people rationalize "padding" a travel expense account. They explain to themselves that the company "owes" them for all the travel they have to do. Or, they reason that the company can afford it since it is such a small amount, and besides, the extra amount means much more to them and they "deserve" it anyway. Such rationalizations are used to make peace with their actions.

These defenses are some of the ways we block ourselves from seeing "current reality." It takes courage to plow through them and clear away the "protections" we put up to preserve our illusions and make ourselves more comfortable. Yet, without a clear view of current reality we are flying blind, at the mercy of circumstances we do not see, unable to take them into account in our planning, thinking, and actions. We end up without a foundation to reach for our dreams.

SUMMARY AND EXERCISES:

Developing the Courage to See Current Reality

". . . And you'll be that glory."

Your ability to hear the "songs" being sung around you, and to know your current song and the impact you have on those around you, is imperative in creating a deep, rich life of love, joy, and success. It means cultivating the second act of courage, seeing current reality. To do so requires the courage to challenge your automatic ways of thinking, feeling, judging, and perceiving. It means being willing to see what is so, even when those around you have a vested interest in not seeing it and in pressuring you to accept their own perception of reality. You foster this courage if you:

First: Resolve today to begin to live your life informed and aware of the reality around you. Establish a foundation from which to move toward your dream by honestly assessing your current reality.

Remember the powerful psychological defense mechanisms that can block your ability to see current reality. Check for the ways you employ these mechanisms, including denial, repression, projection and distortion, and rationalization.

Make a detailed inventory of the way you feel about your life. Consider all aspects of your life. Take the next twenty minutes to write your answers to the following questions, noticing the questions to which you are drawn and also the ones you feel like avoiding:

• What do you most resist hearing or get most upset about when people give you feedback about yourself? Your work? The way you live or behave?

• How is your family and home life?

• How is your work life?

• How are your friendships?

• How is your relationship with nature and the world around you?

• How is your health?

• How do you feel about yourself?

• How is your emotional life?

• What forms the center of your daily life? Is it fulfilling or less than you would like?

• If you could live and experience your life as you truly wanted, what would you be doing differently? How would you feel? (Contrast this to how you are currently living.)

• How is your career? What are the business and market realities you face?

• How are your finances, and how do you feel about them?

• What do you feel in your heart?

Second: Resolve to begin to live from your center, honoring the truth by stating your current reality, both the pleasant and unpleasant aspects. Resolve to tell the truth about the quality and experience of your life, noticing where you tend to avoid what is unpleasant.

Look for opportunities to exercise this act of courage by telling the clear, unvarnished, and unabashed truth about who you are, how you feel, what is going on, and where you stand.

• Start by noticing what you most resist and end up arguing about. Entertain the possibility that you are defending yourself against deeper awareness. Take the viewpoint you most resist and explore it for any truth contained within it.

• Ask someone you trust to help you take a detailed and honest look at how you act, react, and impact others, and how you come across when dealing with others.

• Write down your current reality by describing it from both factual and emotional points of view, and describe how this reality impacts others. Tell the truth with compassion and gentleness. Find someone to share that reality with and let him or her counsel you.

• Interview the key people in your life, personally and professionally. Ask each of them: What am I doing that I should continue doing, and why? What should I stop doing, and why? What should I start doing, and why?

THE THIRD ACT

THE COURAGE TO CONFRONT

"Naught are you but song . . ."

A fundamental law of confrontation states, "When you avoid confronting something today, you create a bigger problem tomorrow." Whenever we back away from confronting a difficult issue, it doesn't disappear or get better on its own. It festers, grows, and undermines our power. When we avoid confronting painful situations or problems in relationships, we inflict damage on our souls and compromise our integrity.

The courage to confront, the third act of courage, is how you "sing." We are shaped as much by what we confront as by what we avoid. Confrontation provides the leverage by which we can move from current reality toward our dream. First, you must develop the courage to dream—to know where you want to go, outline your intentions, and focus your attention. Second, you need the courage to see current reality, to know the foundation from which you start. Third, you must have the courage to confront if you are to move forward. The courage to confront is essential to your power to express yourself and find your true "voice." It frees your spirit and allows you to express the fullness of who you are.

A corollary to the law of confrontation is that pain is inevitable. We may deal with a small issue today and feel a small amount of pain, or we may deal with a greater issue and face greater pain later. When we avoid confronting a problem, it doesn't disappear or go away. Instead, its impact on us grows, the potential pain grows, a pattern unfolds, and, when the inevitable moment of reckoning comes, the pain is ten times worse as a result of our avoidance.

A friend of mine recently told me about the deaths of two of his neighbors that occurred in the space of three months. The first was a 37-year-old man who was rushed to the hospital one afternoon with severe chest pains. The doctors told his wife that her husband had suffered a heart attack. From his hospital bed the man confided that he had been feeling chest pains for the past several months, but he had failed to confront the problem. Instead, he had rationalized away the pain. Within three days he was dead. His wife was left to raise their two young children, and to face a burden of grief and bitterness toward her husband for having been so "thoughtless" in not confronting the pain sooner, or even sharing his problem with her.

The second man, in his early forties and who had been a friend of the first man, witnessed the suffering of the first family. He and his wife extended support to the first man's wife and their two children. Yet, within a few months, he also died from a heart attack, having denied his own chest pains for weeks before his death. He was unable to learn from the tragic mistake of his friend. He also lacked the courage to confront his pain and the potential situation he faced.

Not all failures to confront situations or people end so tragically. However, I have seen many marriages and partnerships break apart, due in part to the failure to confront painful problems early on. This also applies to many failures in careers, teams, and organizations. When we don't confront important issues early on, they compound and grow until the moment of reckoning arrives, bringing even greater pain and consequences than it otherwise would have.

What is so difficult about speaking your truth? What is so daunting about facing a challenging problem or opportunity? Most of us fear that:

- We will have to change or do things differently.

• We will experience pain, rejection, loneliness, or retaliation.

• We will hurt someone else or damage an important relationship.

• We will be "wrong," embarrassed, or humiliated.

During the first few years of marriage, I noticed that when Tina was upset with me, I had a way of somehow making it her fault. I would justify myself by making her wrong. As I developed the courage to see current reality, I began to see a dark and largely unconscious behavior at work. I recognized the behavior as part of an emotional defense I had developed in childhood to protect my self-esteem when I felt attacked or belittled by my parents, teachers, or the new children I met as the Army moved us from place to place each year.

Although I had the courage to see what was going on, I lacked the courage to confront it or share it with Tina. I was afraid she would reject me or take advantage of me if I shared the problem with her. Yet I continued to notice how my acts of self-defense, denial, and blame drove us further apart, eroding our relationship. I practiced telling the truth to myself, confronting the situation in my mind by writing in my journal and reminding myself of what I most deeply valued and wished to experience. It took over a year of preparation and of experiencing our frustrating and ultimately unsatisfying encounters before I could confront the problem I had, in the moment, with integrity.

One Saturday, Tina had just finished confronting me about the mess in the house and my lack of help in dealing with it. At first, I went to my automatic defense, telling her how tired and frustrated I felt about having to work so hard to provide for the family. I began to point out her shortcomings and all the things she wasn't doing for me. Predictably, she became even more upset. Suddenly, a neon sign seemed to light up in front of me that said, "Moment of Truth: She's right!" I felt terror, then guilt, and finally deep remorse and sadness.

Gathering my courage, I stepped back and sat down. I looked past her angry face and saw the frustration and hurt. Taking a deep breath, I confronted the situation. "Sweetheart, you're right. I do make you wrong and end up justifying myself. I'm sorry." She looked surprised and suspicious. I continued, "This is a pattern I've had for many years, and I am ashamed of it. You don't get a fair hearing, and this is not a loving way of relating to you and your concerns. I am stuck and need help in breaking this pattern. You deserve better, and I want better for us."

We then had a breakthrough conversation in which we both confronted the ways we tended to blame each other. What began as a "fight" soon became an emotional sharing and discovery process.

I have seen the pain and damage caused when people avoid confronting problems with themselves and others, not only in the personal arena, but in the professional world as well. For example, an executive with whom I worked was asked by his boss, the president and CEO of the company, to confront an employee who had been causing problems with a key customer. But the executive hated confrontations; they were messy and could spin out of control. He had little practice in, and almost no stomach for, confronting people. He knew the employee had the technical skills to satisfy the customer. He also knew the employee could be a royal pain, often coming across as arrogant or sarcastic.

The executive had been avoiding a confrontation, even though members of his team had complained about the employee in the past. He figured the employee's behavior would not be an issue for long, since his technical abilities and results would eventually outshine his problematic people skills. He also believed that if he gently "suggested" that the employee use more tact with the customer, the employee would "get it" and modify his behavior. Finally, he sent an e-mail to the employee, reminding him of the importance of treating the customer well, including some tips on how to help others feel valued and suggesting the employee work on interpersonal skills.

One month later, the executive was again invited to meet with the president. As he walked into the president's office, he was surprised to see the director of human resources sitting in the office. The president inquired about the employee and asked the executive what he had done to address the problem. At first, the executive spoke in generalities, but the president pressed him for specifics: "Did you call him in for a face-to-face conversation? Did you write him up? Did you ask him for a specific and measurable improvement plan?" Finally, the executive candidly explained that he had sent the employee an e-mail and some suggestions.

The president sat back and asked the director of human resources to speak. The director handed him a memo and asked him to read it. The message was a written warning, charging the executive with endangering the financial well-being of the company. It warned that disciplinary action would follow if he allowed one of his direct reports to alienate an account due to poor professionalism or training.

The executive pleaded, "But I did take action; I warned him in my e-mail. It was his failure, not mine!"

"Your actions were wholly inadequate for addressing the serious behavioral issues of your employee, and you have not responded to the directives I gave you," said the president. "You did not confront the issue nor the person effectively. An e-mail is not the same as a face-to-face discussion. Also, you did not make sure the employee had a development plan to improve how he interacts with others, or to address the concerns and complaints of the customer."

The executive was speechless. He knew the president was right, but he could not concede it. His mind raced through several rationalizations and justifications. After a long silence, he asked the president, "Do you want my resignation?"

After what seemed to him like an eternity, the president responded, "No, I want you to learn from this experience to become a more effective manager. In the meantime, this has shaken my confidence in you, and it will take you some time and effort to rebuild my trust."

After another pause, the executive took an important step: "I will need some help in learning to effectively confront problems with people. Will you help me?" Both the president and the director of human resources agreed to help. The executive, after some hard work, gradually learned to confront others more effectively.

The courage to confront requires you to deal with what is in front of you, to tell your truth with compassion. To do so requires the courage to challenge your automatic ways of thinking, feeling, and perceiving. It also means speaking out about the truth as you see it. My friend and associate, Wayne, is a good example of this. Wayne's father, a rabbi, had always taught that Wayne must marry someone within the faith.

Then Wayne met Debra. The relationship had depth and a power he had never felt before. Unfortunately, Debra wasn't Jewish. So, after realizing he really loved her, Wayne asked her to convert. She thought about it for a while, but decided it wasn't right for her. Finally, he asked Debra to marry him, and she said yes. He knew he would have to confront his father in order to claim the life he wished to have with Debra. It was one of the most difficult things he had ever done. He had always held his father in high esteem and had always sought his approval, but he was sure of instant rejection.

Wayne told his father he had decided to marry Debra and that he hoped his parents would accept her and his decision. His father became upset, and Wayne received the rejection he had anticipated. But he persisted in facing his father and telling him what his relationship with Debra was about. His father withdrew and Wayne began to plan for the marriage, unsure of whether he had lost his father's love.

Finally, the wedding was set, and Wayne's father refused to come. Debra and Wayne had found another

rabbi to conduct the service. At the last minute, Wayne's
father decided to attend. During the ceremony, the rabbi
conducting the service called Wayne's father to come
forward and say the blessing over the couple. He did so;
and father, son, and daughter-in-law embraced.

Sometimes, as with Wayne and his father, a confrontation can lead to a breech in a relationship. Yet, if
what we are called to do, if what we are reaching for,
requires the courage to confront, then we must either
confront or step away from our heart's dream.

Which creates the greater harm: confronting those
we love with something we believe they will reject or
disapprove, or denying our deepest desires? Ultimately, if
we are to make our dreams reality, we must develop the
courage to confront.

One more fundamental truth can be found in confrontation: When we have the courage to confront, we
also create an opportunity to take our relationship to a
deeper level. Though confrontation can be traumatic
and stressful, it can lead to greater connection and
understanding. For example, Wayne's relationship with
his father deepened as Wayne found the courage to
assert himself and claim the life he wished to live. The
act of challenging his father's judgment forced both
Wayne and his father to view their relationship from a
different perspective. The pain led to a deeper dialogue

and, ultimately, to a heartfelt connection that enriched their lives.

The courage to confront is the courage to sing the song you were meant to sing. Yet, that song reveals itself only as we learn to express ourselves and our viewpoints. Learning to confront small situations, to confront when the stakes are not high, prepares you to confront larger issues and to deal with confrontation successfully when the stakes are high.

SUMMARY AND EXERCISES:

Developing the Courage to Confront

"Naught are you but song . . ."

Your ability to "sing the song" you were meant to sing depends on your ability to confront problems and to compassionately speak the truth as you see it. To do so requires the courage to challenge automatic ways of thinking, feeling, and perceiving.

How do you cultivate the courage to confront? Start with reminding yourself about what your life is really about. Review your core values and aspirations, your dreams. Then ask yourself what you want to experience: a greater sense of aliveness, or a sense of diminishment? Then look at your current reality. What in your life do you need to confront? What have you been avoiding? Write down what you wish to create and then outline the people and situations you will have to confront to make your dreams a reality. Here are some other things you can do to create this courage and develop your capacity to "sing out."

First: Resolve to speak the truth with compassion and claim the life you wish to live.

• Ask yourself: What do I avoid speaking about when I am with someone, which I later wish I had said?

• What do you most wish to experience in your life? How do you want to feel about yourself? How do you wish to express your life?

• Make a list of the times you have failed to confront an issue, a situation, or a person. Write down how you felt about yourself and the consequences of not confronting. Notice the price you pay for not confronting.

• List three current people or issues you would like to confront. Describe the benefits you would experience by confronting.

Second: Imagine yourself successfully confronting someone you love.

• Mentally rehearse one of the confrontations; pick one you feel most positive about being able to deal with. Imagine yourself in the situation, saying the crucial words with authority and compassion in your voice. Notice the positive feelings that come with doing this.

• Repeat the mental rehearsal two more times, imagining the words, the way your body would feel, how you would sound. Imagine yourself being successful.

• Now do the same for the other two situations. Feel your innate ability to confront expanding in power and scope.

• Rehearse one more time, focusing on speaking with respect and compassion.

Third: Resolve to confront, with tact and respect, the situation or person you feel would be most ready (and able) to hear you.

• Notice how you feel and what happens. What tone did you use? Were you able to hold your truth and yet remain compassionate? Rehearse how you could have done better and congratulate yourself for having confronted someone or something you needed to confront.

• Look for opportunities to exercise your courage to confront in day-to-day life.

• Take small steps; gently stretch yourself each time, always using compassion and respect.

THE FOURTH ACT

THE COURAGE TO BE CONFRONTED

". . . And as you sing you are."

Learning from criticism is what the fourth act of courage is all about. Instead of viewing the world as a source of threat, we can turn difficult situations into opportunities to become more effective and powerful. Instead of reacting to criticism as an attack, we can appreciate our critics as teachers who have important lessons for us. The courage to be confronted opens doors to incredible learning and greater personal power.

The courage to be confronted is more than just the flip side of the courage to confront. This act is critical to true integrity. Without this act of courage, it is easy to end up off course and out of balance. Once you have developed the courage to formulate your dream, have exercised the courage to see current reality, and have cultivated the courage to confront, you are halfway home.

The fourth act of courage, the courage to be confronted, is where you develop and exercise integrity and demonstrate to others your commitment to live and act from your center. This act allows you to learn from the insights, criticisms, and challenges of others, and enables you to make necessary course corrections.

This act of courage is rare; so few of us have it, and relatively few have seen it modeled effectively. We are constantly on the alert for criticism, and we are prepared to respond to it decisively. Yet our very agility in our self-defense suggests that, by definition, we will learn only slowly and haltingly. We vigorously defend our points of view, our patterns of behaving, and our ways of relating to the world. We also prevent ourselves from living our lives more fully.

When we were young, our parents modeled for us how to give and receive criticism. Now we live and interact in a society that reflects those models. Consider the models we are given: Generally, the models say that whenever we are criticized (translate: "attacked"), we either resist and defend or attack. Occasionally we retreat, but this tactic is more often an avoidance strategy rather than a helpful tool. We see these models used in our homes, offices, in public, and in our social interactions. The models are hideously flawed; they don't work. They create greater pain and suffering, while preventing or seriously inhibiting our ability to learn and grow.

Most of us have been hurt by the words and criticisms of others when we were vulnerable. Consequently, we have built emotional barriers to protect us from criticism. These barriers cause us to go on automatic defense whenever we feel someone is critical of us or something we have done. It takes courage to step out from behind our protective shields and really listen to what is being said.

But it is not enough to confront others, we must also allow others to confront us. In fact, we must invite feedback regarding our impact on others and open ourselves up to criticism and ego blows. We must be willing to become "students" again and learn from others. The willingness to be taught by the criticisms, suggestions, and confrontations of others is an essential act of courage.

The famous and successful playwright Neil Simon once told a radio audience about a time when one of his plays opened off Broadway. He knew something was wrong with the second act, but he just couldn't figure out what it was or how to solve the problem. A local theater critic wrote a scathing review of the play after seeing it. Simon called the critic, who, when Simon identified himself, responded defensively. But Simon shocked him by asking him out to dinner. Over dinner, the playwright asked for more of the critic's observations about the play and scribbled furiously into his notebook as the critic laid out all his thoughts and criticisms. Simon thanked him and paid for his meal. Then, using the man's critique, he rewrote the second act and fine-tuned the first and third acts. The play went on to great success and critical acclaim.

If Neil Simon had lacked the courage to be confronted, to actively seek out criticism, he would have not been able to grow and improve. In fact, he actively sought out criticism as a means of making his work more powerful and effective.

In Defense of Defenselessness

I have another proposition for you: The only real defense is defenselessness. The most powerful and intelligent thing you can do when you feel criticized is set aside the impulse to defend yourself. Instead, vigorously pursue the critic's line of thought and point of view. Seek to understand the context in which the person sees you, or your words and actions. Explore the person's feelings, thoughts, and ideas. Look for the truth of what he or she is saying. Then ask yourself: What possibilities are here for me to become more effective? What can I learn about how I have been thinking and behaving? What does this person need from me in order to give me the best he or she has to give? What would be the most effective thing to do? What can I learn from this criticism? How can I best respond to this criticism to have the impact I want to have?

Defenselessness opens doors, creating possibilities you would have otherwise missed, and it allows you to grow in influence with the other person. On the other hand, what does acting defensively get us? It creates resistance and resentment from those who have the courage to confront us. We merely confirm for them that we are exactly as they see us, and we communicate that we are not willing or able to hear them. This leaves us more vulnerable, more exposed, and less informed. Being defensive, we open ourselves to error and the possibility of failure.

Most of the time, we send out strong verbal and nonverbal messages to others that say, "Don't confront me; cater to my ego." We deflect the information that would allow us to learn more quickly and interact with others more gracefully and effectively. In our automatic, well-rehearsed, and largely unconscious defenses, we create more pain and suffering for ourselves than we suspect, and we remain blind to the consequences.

According to a recent article in the *Wall Street Journal*, most of us believe it is unwise to be completely honest with our boss. If we are asked to give an honest, candid evaluation of our boss's strengths and weaknesses, we generally lie. After all, the ego is a fragile thing, and the ego of a boss is particularly fragile. And, if we are completely honest and open, we will likely be punished later on. Therefore it should come as no surprise that most executives are dismayed by what those who work for them say about their strengths and weaknesses when that feedback is supplied anonymously. The fact that they are caught by surprise and have to struggle to digest the information is revealing in itself. It forms an indictment of our models for handling criticism and confrontation: Because of how we process criticism, we have become learning impaired, and our management and leadership abilities show only slight improvement over time.

But it is not only in our corporate offices that the courage to be confronted is lacking. As a marriage and family therapist I saw many individuals, couples, and families damaged by their unwillingness to be confront-ed, or even to hear the criticisms, from those they loved and who loved them. I saw firsthand the damage and pain these defensive patterns created.

A family once came to me for help in dealing with their "troubled" 16-year-old daughter. Mother and father were at their wits' end, and the family—the three of them, plus a six-year-old son—was in constant turmoil. The girl, whom I'll call Sally, was angry, hostile, and verbally abusive, and she had recently been suspended from school for fighting. Her mother and father, Elizabeth and Jim, told me what they considered to be her problem behaviors and described how they had dealt with her. When I asked Sally what she thought, she glared at me and wouldn't speak. Elizabeth tried to prod her, but Sally remained silent. Jim appeared angry, yet I saw redness around his eyes and sensed a great sadness. He sat with folded arms, watching his wife.

After listening to them for a while, I asked Elizabeth if I could say something to Sally. She nodded, never taking her eyes off of her daughter. I said, "Sally, you seem to have a lot bottled up inside of you. I want you to listen carefully to what I will say. No one has ever said anything like this to you before. Are you ready?"

Sally turned and looked at me for the first time. She appeared curious, and a bit suspicious, but, after a moment of silence, she nodded. I said, "Sally, I think it's very brave of you to try to protect your parents. You are working very hard at it, and you must be exhausted." Her eyes opened wide, and she began to cry. Her parents stared at me: Jim with surprise, and Elizabeth with what appeared to be rage. Sally, wiping her eyes, sobbed.

I continued, "It must be very hard for you to take so much upon yourself, but I think it's time you let your parents take care of themselves. You need to take care of Sally, and you have really neglected her. You must feel lonely, sad, and angry about all this." Sally nodded, her whole face softened, and the anger seemed to melt from her body. Her father saw the change, and a faint smile formed at the corner of his mouth, but Elizabeth began to look angry.

I asked Jim to tell me what my words had meant to him. He looked first at me, and then at his angry wife. Finally, he found the courage to speak in spite of his wife's anger and disapproval. "It just made sense. I think you were telling her that she isn't responsible for the problems between me and my wife."

Elizabeth looked even more furious. "What the hell are you talking about?" she asked. "This is about Sally, not us!"

Jim replied, "No, I think it's about you and me, and Sally has been caught in the middle."

His wife turned to me and started to say something laced with energy, but her daughter interrupted saying, "Mama, I'm sorry to have been so difficult. But I have been very mad at you and Papa. You are so unhappy, and it is so painful to watch." Sally cried as she said these words. Her mother's mouth dropped open, speechless.

I spoke, "It was evident from your interactions that you have had a great deal of tension in your marriage. Jim seems defeated and sad. Elizabeth, you seem angry and unhappy. Sally has been acting out the anger and frustration between the two of you, in addition to working out the challenges of adolescence. She has been the glue that held you together, but the burden is now too heavy for her. You two need to face the problems and challenges in your marriage, and Sally needs to take care of herself."

Jim sighed, "Elizabeth, I can hear the truth in what he's saying. Can you?"

Elizabeth looked at him as her tears began to flow, and said, "I wasn't aware you were so unhappy with me!"

"I think it's more that you are unhappy with me," he replied. "That's what I have felt, and because of it, I have withdrawn and closed down."

This breakthrough eventually led to a revitalized marriage for Jim and Elizabeth, and a much more rewarding life for Sally. The hardest part was helping Elizabeth get to the point where she could be confronted by those who loved her. She had blocked out her husband's complaints and the criticisms of her daughter. She had been the "power broker" in the family, and, as long as she would not hear what others had to say, all that was left for them was to withdraw and shut down, as her husband had; or to rebel, as her daughter had. But, as soon as Elizabeth made it "safe" for them to speak up, without punishing them for their opinions, their marriage and family life improved dramatically.

In the process of defending ourselves from confrontations with others, in denying their perceptions, we do violence both to them and to ourselves. We block their attempts to express their truths. We hurt others by withdrawing, attacking, or discounting their sense of reality, and we mar our own ability to connect with others and learn how we impact others.

What gets in the way? Several things reinforce our old, failed models of defensiveness and prevent us from becoming more effective in dealing with criticism. They include:

- Past wounds
- Future projections
- Mistaking form for substance

Past Wounds

Past wounds come from experiences in your personal history when you felt hurt or damaged by the actions, inactions, or words of others. If these experiences were powerful enough initially, or if they were repeated, the equivalent of scar tissue would form on the psyche. This scar tissue is very sensitive to any stimulation that remotely resembles the past experience. As people confront us with their view of reality, especially if the confrontation is critical of us or our behavior, our scar tissue is often disturbed. We feel pain, threatened, and we automatically become defensive. These defensive patterns, which we developed to help us deal with pain in our lives, are largely automatic processes that can "take over" unless we actively inhibit them and make conscious choices in the moment.

In Sally's case, her mother, Elizabeth, had come from a family with a verbally abusive father. She had deep scars from being told repeatedly that she wasn't "worth a damn." She had developed powerful defenses of denial, rationalization, and counterattacks. Her defenses were activated any time those close to her offered criticism or challenged her assumptions. She ruled her family with ferocious tenacity, tolerating no confrontation from anyone. But her defenses, which had served her well in childhood, were now destroying her marriage and her relationship with her daughter.

Future Projections

Future projections are products of our God-like power to imagine the future, and to create images and story lines for events that may or may not happen. These projections are really flights of fantasy we engage in, in which we make mountains out of molehills and disasters out of irritations. Sometimes, when we allow our imaginations to run wild, we can create in our minds scenes of pleasure and success. But, more often, especially when we are threatened, we create scenes of pain and suffering. In these scenarios, we imagine ourselves being hurt or taken advantage of.

These future projections create such vivid images of the way we are, or the way things ought to be, that we deflect feedback from others. We get so caught up in living out some future possibility, we do not hear the concerns of those right in front of us. These images are very appealing. They convince us that everything will turn out great, if only we can make things go exactly our way. In these circumstances we are likely to block-out, resist, or even become hostile to anyone offering feedback that runs counter to our preconceptions of how things should be.

When we escape into future fantasies or create cat-astrophic images, we no longer hear or respond to the needs and concerns of others. We remove ourselves from the possibility of learning from feedback. We make ourselves unavailable, and ironically, we fail to antici-pate the real outcome. It takes courage to challenge these projections, for, in the thick of it, they appear absolutely true.

Mistaking Form for Substance

It is easy to forget ourselves, to mistake symbols for reality. We love each symbol, whether it's a piece of jewelry, a company logo, or another status symbol. When we mistake these symbols for the real substance, we end up like the man who went to a five-star restaurant, read the menu, and, with mouth watering, ate the menu! Then he complained about the dry and tasteless meal!

Every day, many of us figuratively eat the menu instead of the meal. When those around us do not confront or criticize us, we begin to feel secure that we have their support. In truth, all we've done is disconnect the warning lights. We "eat the menu" rather than the meal. But, in human relationships, the "meal" of life is spiced with criticism and confrontation.

I have worked with many people involved in blocked or problematic relationships as they tried to work through challenging professional assignments, or as couples struggled to reconnect their relationships during difficult times. I have found that many people believe criticism and confrontation are signs of serious problems, or even of a failed relationship. Negative feedback and negative reactions to feedback are often taken as signs of the other person's "personality problem" or that something is just "wrong" between them.

In fact, criticism and confrontation indicate there is a relationship! Consider the times in which you, yourself, struggled to reach a decision within your own mind; yet, you probably did not storm off in anger at yourself in those instances. After all, your best interests are most easily negotiated with yourself. And we know that whenever we are in a relationship with another person for a significant length of time, we can expect to face criticism and confrontation.

To be in a relationship in which something important is required is to be at once in a paradoxical state of challenge, harmony, and accommodation. A dynamic, shifting balance between these three states is to be found in any vital relationship. In fact, such a state is required in professional teamwork, as well as in loving, intimate relationships. The smooth flow between harmoniously connecting, working, and supporting each other is often troubled by challenges, resistance, and confrontations, which are then balanced by accommodation, negotiation, and occasionally, letting go. Both sides must participate in each area.

When we expect this dynamic tension, understanding that it is part of any long-term relationship, we are better prepared to face these tensions when they occur, working with the other person to learn and grow. Confrontations are opportunities for making breakthroughs in our own thinking, as well as in living and working with others. They can become creative moments in which intense and compressed learning can occur.

For me, I discovered the secret to confrontation in a painful, yet powerful life experience. I was 25 years old and managing a crisis center in North Carolina. I had been in my job for about six months and had assumed control of the center, which was in turmoil. The center was under contract with the county mental health center to be open 24 hours a day, seven days a week, but we didn't have adequate volunteers to staff the schedule, nor did we have proper accounting and reporting to satisfy the contract. Since this was my first full-time job as a professional, I overcompensated. I threw myself into a major recruitment and training effort, adding 50 volunteers to our roster and training them within six months. I revamped our reporting process and prepared monthly reports, which were submitted to the mental health center.

While I was upgrading the crisis center, I offered my services to other county agencies. I worked with local elementary and high school authorities to craft an education program for their drug prevention and life learning curriculum. I co-sponsored a day in the park, planning events, lectures, counseling, and offering information about the crisis center to the public. I also invited the county commissioners to an open house, where they could meet the volunteers and learn about our work at the crisis center. I felt I had accomplished many things, and I hoped I could demonstrate this to the county commissioners at the open house.

After six months as director, I received a letter from the area director of the four-county mental health center, which managed the county mental health center to whom my center reported, serving notice that he was canceling our contract and demanding my immediate dismissal. I was devastated. I read and re-read the letter in total disbelief. Additionally, all my past wounds were activated. All the ways I had ever heard that I wasn't good enough, or that I didn't measure up, and all the criticism I had ever received, came to the surface.

I finally stopped my "catastrophizing" and went into a "warrior" mode. First, I figured that if the charges were true (and I believed they weren't), it would not be my word against his, but my evidence against his evidence. I needed to take the confrontation, and, instead of denying it and arguing with him, I would simply ask for an impartial third party to investigate. At any rate, I knew intuitively that the charges needed to be fully embraced and investigated. I knew that a CYA (cover your "assets") attitude had led others to big problems throughout human history. I decided that I would either hang from being too frank and open, or be completely exonerated.

Once I embraced the confrontation, I felt calmer. I called the state drug authority in Raleigh and spoke to the administrator, whom I had met several times and whose counsel I valued. I reviewed the letter with him and asked if he would lead an investigation to either prove or disprove the charges. He was very accommodating and said that he would attend to the investigation within the next few days. He also said he would write to the area director to inform him of the investigation and to ask for any evidence that might support his allegations.

Then I called the director of the Parks and Recreation department, the director of the school curriculum development effort, and the chairman of the crisis center's board of directors to ask for their cooperation in the investigation and to share their candid impressions of working with me and my staff in a letter. Each of them did so, and the crisis center chairman also proposed to call a meeting of the board to review the charges and discuss a response.

As a courtesy, I called the chairman of the county commissioners, since he had expressed strong interest in our work when he attended the open house. I wanted him to hear the news from me, rather than from a third party, and I told him I had asked for a full investigation. He was generous in his comments and offered support. I asked him to check with various county executives with whom I had worked. He agreed and also offered to share his impressions with the investigators.

Finally, I called the area director's office and found out he happened to be visiting the nearby county mental health center that day, observing the center's care and treatment of patients. Quickly, I grabbed the six monthly reports I had sent to the director of the county center, and drove to the clinic. I waited in the reception area, unannounced, to see if I could talk to him for five minutes.

Moments later, the director emerged with a file in his hand and agreed to see me. I stepped forward and said, "I just received your letter, and . . ." He cut me off and began yelling at me in front of a room full of patients. I don't remember much of what he said; I felt shocked and overpowered by his domineering personality and physical presence, and intimidated by his credentials.

When he stopped yelling, with trembling knees I spoke again, "Sir, I believe you have been misinformed, and I only want to . . ." He cut me off again.

Then, locking my knees and speaking through my fear, I said, "I have asked the state drug authority for a full investigation of the charges and have asked the county commissioners for a hearing."

Suddenly, all the fire went out of him and he replied in a mild, even friendly tone, "Now, now, you didn't need to do that; you should have just talked with me first."

All my fear evaporated. I sensed the balance of power had shifted. I handed him the stack of reports, six inches thick, and said, "Here are the reports I have been send-ing—six reports for six months. Perhaps you have not seen them, and so you were misinformed. Anyway, I wanted you to know I take your charges very seriously."

In a cordial tone he replied, "Mr. Staub, I'm sure we can work this out, but now isn't the time. Let me arrange a lunch with you and me and the director of the county center, and we can discuss the whole matter. How about tomorrow?" I agreed and thanked him for being willing to talk with me. We shook hands and I left.

A week later, the crisis center received news that the charges had been disproved by the investigating committee. Also, endorsements from all over the coun-ty poured in from key officials, and the area director apologized. All the work my staff and I had done had now been acknowledged, and we felt relieved.

This confrontation forced me to dig deeply into my soul to find the proper response and courage to embrace and explore the area director's point of view. I had also been fortunate to receive some good advice prior to taking the job at the crisis center from Mansfield Elmore, the director of the Alcohol and Drug Treatment Center in a nearby county. He said, "Staub, if you raise the dead but it isn't documented, you haven't done anything in the eyes of the world." So I had carefully documented each call, patient, and service we performed prior to the ordeal. Thus, I entered the confrontation armed with good work, solid documentation, and a network of allies.

I learned it is much easier to let confrontation in, and to respond positively, when you have a strong support network. It is easier to hear criticism when we know we have support for who we are and what we have done. This helps build our courage, and allows us to respond more creatively and openly when challenged, criticized, or confronted.

SUMMARY AND EXERCISES:

Developing the Courage to Be Confronted

". . . And as you sing you are."

Your ability to learn from criticism and confrontation depends on your capacity to embrace confrontation instead of relying on automatic defenses. This requires that you:

1. Understand that to be in a relationship is to face regular criticism and confrontation. This is part of the nature of "relating."

2. Develop a support network to help you respond to criticism and confrontation without resorting to your automatic defenses. Whenever you do resort to your automatic defenses, have people around you who can compassionately help and encourage you to open up.

3. Give up the need to be "right." This means you must develop your self-esteem and inner wisdom to the point where you know it is more important to learn to relate to others and win than to be "right."

4. Realize that the criticism that most upsets you may be an arrow pointing directly at your ability to learn and grow.

Here are some things you can do to create this courage and develop your capacity to let yourself be taught.

First: Resolve to learn from others when they criticize or confront you. The only barriers to learning are the scar tissues on our egos, caused by old wounds, future projections, and mistaking form for substance.

• Notice what kinds of criticism or confrontation activate your automatic defenses. Are these triggered by criticism about your abilities, thoughts, appearance, actions, expressions, or your work? Does any form of confrontation and criticism disturb you?

• Look for the root of your defensive patterns. Once you see how you go on "automatic" and when, look for what you say to yourself, in either words or images, which feeds that defensive response.

Second: Resolve to embrace the criticisms and confrontations you receive. Remember, safety lies in being defenseless. You will always be more hurt by defending than by opening yourself up to feedback.

• Take each criticism and confrontation as an opportunity to be the student, to learn more about yourself and the workings of your own mind and heart, as well as those of others.

• Consider each confrontation as an opportunity to understand how the other person's mind and heart work, and how he or she sees the world. See it as an opportunity to understand the other person better, and, if you wish, to build a stronger relationship.

Third: Seek out opportunities for receiving criticism and confrontation.

• Ask yourself, "What do I think needs defending? Is it worth the energy I am expending to defend it?"

• Ask others to practice with you in giving and receiving confrontational messages.

• Practice listening with your heart as well as your head; learn to be suspicious of any automatic defenses you use.

• Create a network of relationships in which those around you are supportive, compassionate, and honest enough to help you "see" when you are getting trapped in automatic, pre-programmed ways of thinking, acting, and dealing with others.

• Notice any time you feel heavily invested in "being right"; practice giving up the need to be right. Turn your attention to why you feel you need to be right and use this discovery to expand your mind and soul.

• Be gentle with yourself. When you feel most defensive, it is likely when you most need to be encouraging and kind with yourself. Use the defensive feeling as a tracking device to locate where you have been blocking your ability to learn. You will almost always find a fear behind the defense. Gently address this fear by remaining open and encouraging yourself.

THE FIFTH ACT

THE COURAGE TO LEARN AND GROW

*"You thought you were the teacher,
but find you are the taught."*

The courage to learn and grow is the commitment to challenge your assumptions, to slay your own sacred cows. It means moving from the certainty of what you know to the ambiguous ground of uncertainty and doubt. It takes great courage to let go of the known and seek new understandings, self-definitions, and ways of being and acting.

The courage to learn and grow is essentially the courage to go beyond the first impulse that comes to you when you are challenged or in doubt or fear. It requires the willingness to face the unknown and the untried. It requires looking deep into your heart and soul, and letting go of the need to be right and to stay in control. It is found when we step into ambiguity and explore the unknown. It opens the way to enhanced learning, and to more powerful and effective ways of relating to the world. As the visionary poet William Blake observed, "Knowledge is only the ratio of what is known. The ratio of what is known will change as we learn more. To learn means to let go of the known and let divine imagination guide us."

Chris Argyris has written extensively on how smart people stop learning, because of their successful achievements. They get stuck in being "right," and remain heavily invested in the dead weight of what worked for them in the past. His studies show that we get stuck in behaviors that we believe contributed to our success. We become attached to, even rigid about, particular ways of thinking, acting, and interacting. This may be fine if the old patterns continue to fit and serve the changing world, and continue to work effectively with new processes, relationships, or roles. But when they don't, which is often the case, we experience loss and failure, often blaming others while we hold tightly to our cherished beliefs and behaviors.

Thus, some of the most intelligent and successful people, unless they are particularly vigilant, are apt to be the slowest learners. Their ability to learn is hampered by the baggage they carry as the "requirements" of success, which they pin to past patterns. I compare this to driving a car while only looking in the rearview mirror.

What happens to individuals also happens to families, teams, and organizations. According to Andy Grove, chief executive officer of Intel, "Only the paranoid survive." Just as an individual can become stuck in past behaviors, so can organizations. Grove and other successful leaders are keenly aware of the dangers of success and the complacency and addiction people often find in doing things "the right way," because of that success.

We place ourselves in needless danger when we do not remain vigilantly aware of our need to grow and change, and when we don't allow ourselves to let go of behaviors that have led to success. We must see current reality and find the courage to learn and grow by stepping into new, untried, and possibly ambiguous situations. When we fail to exercise this act of courage, we begin down a slippery slope of complacency, riding the sled of unchallenged assumptions. This can be particularly dangerous when we wear a blindfold of denial.

Compounding this, we humans have two strong needs that impact our abilities to learn and grow: The first need is to predict what is going to happen in our world, particularly in relation to things around us. The second need is to control the results of the first need. Together, these needs demand a high level of certainty about what is "right" and about how we can control developments in our lives. If we are not careful, these needs, and the impulses that go with them, often result in an addiction to being "right."

This addiction plays itself out in many ways. We resist views and ideas that threaten our picture of how things are. The addiction is so strong we may sabotage ourselves and damage the things that are most precious to us. Sadly, many of us would rather be "right" than happy. In the words of an old cigarette advertisement, we would "rather fight than switch" to different ways of thinking, acting, or relating to others. We become trapped in our need to be "right."

I have seen people sacrifice their families, careers, teams, and even whole organizations by arguing over who is right—all for the sake of not being wrong. They would rather be right than win! By being "right," they miss out on creating loving and enjoyable relationships.

This addiction begins when we mistake form for substance, described in the preceding chapter. It is easy to mistake winning an argument or having others capitulate to our view as what is important, but we often do not notice when we have damaged relationships or traveled down a path which has less to offer. Many times, others allow us to be "right" and win the small battles, even as we lose larger and more vital issues that would have constituted major life victories.

Psychologists have studied this same phenomenon in laboratory rats. The study of rats can shed some light on how the human mind works and offers suggestions about why we behave the way we do. In one interesting study, a rat is placed in a maze with at least three different paths, each ending in a different "den" or resting place. The scientist places something, such as a piece of cheese, in one of the dens, and the rat is placed at the beginning of the maze and is allowed to explore.

At first, the rat explores the maze slowly, but it soon becomes more eager. It goes down the first tunnel, finding nothing of interest. It then finds its way back and explores the next tunnel, and so forth, until by accident, it finds the path that leads to the cheese. The rat becomes excited and gets to eat some of the cheese. The scientist then promptly places the rat at the start of the maze. Each time, the rat moves faster in its explorations and its ability to locate the cheese. This process is repeated until the rat "knows" where the cheese is, and finds it quickly every time.

At this point, the scientist places the cheese in a different den, and the rat is no longer able to find the cheese. The rat spent a lot of time and energy to learn where the cheese was, and it was there every time, but now it's gone. So, from the rat's perspective, it should still be there! The rat will continue to seek the cheese in the same place for some time.

But the main difference between rats and most humans is that rats will eventually get it through their small heads that the cheese must be somewhere else. They will explore other tunnels until they find the new location. Rats place very little importance on being "right"; they only want the cheese.

Humans, on the other hand, "know" the cheese is supposed to be there, and will become self-righteous about this knowledge. They continue to insist that the cheese will eventually show up if only they can work harder, or faster, or use more money, or get more people to agree on where the cheese is supposed to be. After all, "It has always been here; it should be here, and it soon will be here!"

By insisting on being "right," we don't explore other paths, and we end up missing out on the real thing. We mistake the form of being "right" for the real experience of getting the "cheese"—what we really want, and what will sustain our hearts and feed our souls. The "cheese," in human terms, is loving and being loved by others, or a sense of accomplishment and personal mastery, or winning and getting ahead in life. It is getting what you really want, as opposed to what you think you "ought" to have. It is the capacity to learn how to learn faster and better. It is increased self-confidence, personal enjoyment, and success.

The need to be right can blind us to new ways of thinking, acting, and interacting. We continue to walk dead-end paths getting the dregs of what once might have been, but knowing, by golly, that we are right! We all do it at times, no matter how smart we are. We do things we know from experience will not work, but, by maintaining the fiction of being right we somehow convince ourselves we are winning in life, even as satisfaction, love, and success slip through our hands.

In my bachelor days, my best friend and I went on a vacation to Jamaica. It was the first time either of us had experienced a tropical island, and we thoroughly enjoyed it. On our return trip, we passed through the Atlanta airport. He had borrowed some money from me in Jamaica, and we were settling accounts as we walked to our connecting flight.

I told him he owed me five dollars for a loan at one of the open air markets. My friend, who tended to be generous with anything but money, argued with me. He told me he didn't owe me five dollars; at most it was only fifty cents. Usually, I would have simply given in to avoid an argument. After all, it was only five dollars, and the amount was not really important to me. But, in that moment, I decided to stick by what I knew was right. He owed me five dollars. I was totally willing to let him keep it, but I wanted him to acknowledge I had given him the money.

He continued to argue with me and mentioned other transactions where we had exchanged money during the week. I had kept a tab of the transactions and began, with some anger, to review them with him. Surprised at my anger and tenacity, he became angry in return.

I was tired of hassling with my "best friend" about money issues; I was fighting for the "principle" of the matter and wanted him to acknowledge I was right. This time, I was not going to simply accommodate his "neurotic pattern." My friend, on the other hand, was tired of feeling "judged" by me and fought back against my self-righteousness. The conversation became increasingly unpleasant and heated.

As I delivered my loud sermon to his angry and rigid face, I paused; a deeper impulse within me stirred. I let the impulse surface, and I was surprised at how much pain I was feeling. As I opened up to the pain, everything seemed changed in an instant. I felt my anger evaporate, and I felt tears well up in my eyes. The pain felt like layers of frozen hurt, avalanching into grief. I looked at him and let the emotions flow as I spoke from my heart instead of my pride.

Even as I spoke, I felt gratitude for having released the burden I had been carrying. Along with this inner freedom came a deep feeling of aliveness. I spoke softly, "I can't believe a few dollars is more important to you than our friendship. Our friendship is more important to me than the money. What I really feel is that I don't matter much as a friend."

My friend's face changed the instant he heard the new tone in my voice. I noticed tears in his eyes as he listened. Then he spoke with sadness and hurt from his own heart, "I'm sorry you feel hurt. It's just that you had this old look on your face of being so much better than me, and you sounded so judgmental of me, like I was contemptible. That look and tone have hurt me many times in our friendship." I was completely receptive to his words and his feelings. They resonated with mine and, at the same time, gave me information and insight I had never had before.

The new insights and awareness washed over me so powerfully that I could not speak for a while. I saw how, over years of childhood, I had constructed a defense of "superior judgment" as a way of dealing with my father's anger and disapproval. And I saw that I'd actually had power over my father when I used it. Now I began to see how it must have injured and hurt him, even as it had hurt others, including my friend.

In the days that followed, I put this new awareness to use, noticing my face and tone of voice in ways I never had before. I could now tell when I was going on automatic defense, feeling my face assume an old aspect of judgment and condescension. The strange thing was that the facial movements and tone were familiar, as if I had been aware of them all along, but only now had my heart opened enough to really notice. It was a revelation of how powerfully the mind, driven by ego, can block out the obvious.

My tone of voice also began to convey a world of information to me, and I saw how I had used it occasionally to put others on the defensive to protect myself from threats. This meant I could now consciously change my behavior instead of defending it. I could share, or at least examine, the hurt and then respond in a way that was more loving and effective. I experienced a profound improvement in my friendships and, God be praised, in my relationship with my father.

My life, which had felt good before, became much more rich and loving, and I felt myself growing and learning at an accelerated rate. It was wonderful. All I had to do was let go of my need to be "right." It was as if a door had been shut in my psyche, but was now opened, leading to a garden of beauty in which more loving and joyful relationships were blooming.

What had been required of me in the Atlanta airport was the courage to learn and grow, which, as it turns out, is also the courage to face the obvious. I had to:

1. Choose to learn in the moment.
2. Be curious, wishing to learn what the deeper impulse was.
3. Let go of what I "knew."
4. Let go of being "right."
5. Step into ambiguity.
6. Listen with an open heart.

These keys have helped me again and again to find the courage to learn and grow. Perhaps the fundamental decision is that of choosing the path of heart versus the path of personality and ego.

The path of heart is the path of living based on a commitment to being fully alive. This path is full of joy, self-expression, and an enhanced relationship with the world. This path brings out our deep, innate curiosity and opens the floodgates of compassion and of enlarged perspectives on life and self. As the *Tao Te Ching* says, "Consider the world as yourself, and you will fear nothing."

SUMMARY AND EXERCISES:

Developing the Courage to Learn and Grow

*"You thought you were the teacher,
but find you are the taught."*

The courage to learn and grow requires being willing to suspend what we know, and to break our addiction to being "right." Without it, we block ourselves from the ability to learn gracefully and quickly. We get bogged down in defensive maneuvers, proving others wrong, or spending great energy to maintain our positions and ways of thinking. This slows the learning process and makes us vulnerable to the deadly disease "hardening of the categories," which can be fatal in marriages, careers, or organizations that fail to learn and grow.

First: Make the commitment to face your fears of letting go of "certainty" and the need to be "right." Decide you will get more out of life by continuing to learn and grow, by lightening your load and setting down the heavy legacy of proving yourself right and resisting new views.

• Let go of expecting the world to conform to your expectations; instead, meet the world where it is, observing and learning from what is so.

- Challenge yourself to look at the world from different perspectives and new assumptions.

- Notice whenever you go on "automatic" and start defending or arguing your opinions.

- Watch, over a period of several weeks, whenever you start feeling "righteous" or expend your energy to prove yourself right.

Second: Commit to live from a more open learning approach. The following process will help:

- Choose to learn in the moment. Let the moment be your teacher and guide. Look at what is immediately before you, not at memories or rehearsed responses and behaviors.

- Be curious; seek what the deeper impulse might be. Look for what is moving deeply in your soul, not in the mechanics of your personality. Ask yourself, "What am I feeling at my core? What might others be feeling, if I get beyond my initial interpretations?"

- Let go of what you think you "know." Certainty is like rigor mortis for the soul, as well as the mind. What if you have been wrong in the way you've put something together? What if there is a more loving and powerful way of seeing and understanding what is going on?

- Learn to treat your judgments with suspicion. See if you can use descriptive language or questioning to understand from a deeper and more powerful place. If you are successful, you will see at least three different options for responding to and dealing with a person or situation. You will be more open to interaction and will use your power more effectively.

• Step into ambiguity. Focus on the "shades of gray." Notice how often your thinking is automatic and computer-like: "right versus wrong," "black versus white," "yes versus no," "off versus on," and so forth. Argue the other side of your position first. Then look to see if a third perspective can be found which encompasses the first two alternatives you see. Look for the integrative whole. What can you learn from this larger perspective?

• Listen with an open heart. Work to see the essential self, the heart of the person with whom you're dealing. Feel what he or she is feeling. Listen deeply to your heart and respond first by feeling, then by looking deep into your soul before responding.

THE SIXTH ACT

THE COURAGE TO BE VULNERABLE, TO LOVE

*"You thought you were the seeker,
and find you are the sought."*

The greatest gift you have to give is yourself. There is no substitute. Are you courageous enough to be loved by others for who you are? To be fully yourself? To be needed? To own the unique gifts you bring to your work, your family, and your life? Are you courageous enough to realize you are "the sought"?

The courage to be vulnerable, to care, to love, is essentially the willingness to be penetrated by life and by the genuine needs of others. It is the great act of courage in which you open your eyes to the fact that you and your portfolio of gifts, talents, and unique way of being are what is ultimately sought by those around you.

We have all been hurt, at times, by those we love, by someone we trusted, or by disappointments, mistakes, accidents, and personal attacks. We all know what it feels like to be taken advantage of, to lose a loved one, or to experience a broken heart. Still, the choice to remain vulnerable, to be open to love, requires courage. This requires choosing the deepest part of our heart as the center, as our compass and guide as we live our lives and do our work.

To choose the deepest part of our heart as our center is to challenge our old patterns of protecting ourselves, our automatic and pre-recorded ways of acting and responding to others. Fear and anger can block us. It takes courage to walk through fear and anger and to remain open and available to life and those around us. To live our lives wholeheartedly means to practice the courage of opening up, of making ourselves present, of listening and attending to the needs, weaknesses, gifts, and strengths of those with whom we live and work.

When I was in graduate school, my last internship was at the VA hospital in Durham, North Carolina. I was assigned to floor 4-B, thoracic and general surgery. Out of all the patients and families with whom I worked, one person in particular stands out. He was a veteran of World War II, dying from esophageal cancer. He could no longer talk, and his meals were given by a stomach tube, since nothing could pass the swollen, scarred remnants of his esophagus.

His wife, daughter, and the daughter's husband traveled more than three hours by car to see him each week, staying in town on weekends to be with him. He was emaciated and wasting away, slipping in and out of consciousness. I was moved by the love, longing, and intense grief expressed by the mother and her daughter. He, on the other hand, lay in the bed, holding their hands, nodding at them, and smiling or crying as they talked. His eyes were already seeing another world, but a kindness and love poured from his eyes when he gazed at his family.

During the few short weeks I knew him, I could see him growing weaker every day. I was frightened by the prospect of witnessing his impending death, but I prayed for courage and felt I should be there to support him and his family. In the process, I came to love and admire them.

When he died, I was in the room, along with his wife and daughter. He had been lapsing in and out of consciousness for days, the conscious moments becoming increasingly brief and infrequent. The last time he opened his eyes, I was there as he lifted his finger and his wife took his hand and caressed it. She lifted it to her lips and kissed his hand with such tenderness that I felt tears welling in my eyes. As she cried, her daughter reached over and took her parents' hands in hers. She kissed each hand and covered them with her hair as she cried. I saw the man's eyes flutter and close for what would be the last time. His breathing became labored and rough. The attending nurse suggested they speak to him, saying he would probably still hear them. They hesitated, and I added my encouragement that they tell him what they most wanted him to hear.

They told him simply, clearly, and with many tears, how much they loved him, and what a wonderful father and generous man he was. They asked him to remember them in heaven. His breathing became labored and, in the next ten minutes, ceased completely. Before the nurse led them away minutes later, the man's wife held his hand, stretching out the contact, slid her fingers reluctantly across his hand, and then slowly, and with great tenderness, laid his hand on the bed. Covering her face with her hand, she was led away with her daughter's arms around her.

In the intensity of that moment, I watched as she struggled to let go of his hand, and I understood that all we ever love, all we ever have, will be taken from us by death. We pay a great price, indeed, for loving others and being open to pain. Yet, I felt incredible gratitude and inspiration in that moment. I knew I would ultimately say good-bye to all I loved. With brilliant clarity, I felt how precious this moment was, not only for the mother and daughter, but for me.

The words came to mind, "Choose love and love completely. Have what you have, and be fully present." I had witnessed the pain and the joy of being penetrated by love, of being really loved, and of loving another person. I knew then that to love, with the awareness of inevitable loss, requires great courage. It struck me that every true act of love is an act of courage.

It is impossible to love, to really give it or to receive it, if we are not vulnerable. Our very attempts to protect ourselves from hurt—by defending, arguing, withdrawing, and otherwise restricting our expressions of love—block us from showing and receiving love. We cut ourselves off from matters of the heart and then feel powerful longings for connection and meaning in life. Our emotional defenses are driven by the healthy desire to protect ourselves from pain and loss. But these defenses imprison our hearts, shutting us off from that which nourishes us. Our very attempts to protect ourselves from hurt guarantee that we will experience more hurt.

A woman once came to me for therapy. She was highly intelligent, graceful, and very beautiful. Her husband adored her, her friends admired her, and she had been on a satisfying spiritual quest. But she had recently become stuck and felt emotionally blocked. What's worse, she realized that she had never allowed herself to receive the admiration or love of others. She felt great loneliness and longing, and a shroud of emptiness wrapped her broken heart.

As we worked, it became apparent that she had made the decision, unconsciously, to not enjoy what she had. She would not allow herself to need anything or anyone. She kept herself apart from others, including her husband, to protect herself from feeling vulnerable. To her, this meant she could not be hurt because she was protecting her heart from being broken. If anything happened to someone she loved, she believed it would not hurt as badly. "Besides," she said as we uncovered the pattern, "what you won't let in, can't hurt you!"

But the truth was that the very act of withholding love meant she couldn't really enjoy what she had. By denying herself the joy of being open and loving with others, she felt great emptiness and loss. I asked her to imagine her deathbed and to consider how she would feel about herself and her life if she continued this behavior. She began to sob, feeling a sense of loss and loneliness, and said. "Why, I never really 'had' what I had; I blew it! By protecting my heart, I walled myself off from those who were most important to me."

I told her she was like the woman who went to a feast, but only ate crumbs from the table, thinking she wouldn't regret her reluctance when the feast was gone: She was afraid of getting what she most wanted and then losing it or being disappointed by the consequences of indulging. In minimizing the possibility of pain, she was avoiding what she most wanted.

She understood intuitively the emotional cost she paid in guarding and protecting her heart. The protective behavior, created as a means of dealing with her over-critical mother and then amplified when her beloved grandfather died, had now become a wall to keep her emotions inside. She had decided never to let herself be hurt again, and it would take great courage for her to re-engage her life at the heart level, to allow love and feelings for others to return to the surface.

What You Seek Also Seeks You

Here is a wonderful secret: What you are most deeply looking for in life is also, with great loyalty and dedication, seeking you. You are the sought! Love is seeking you just as you seek it. What you long for is coming to you, if you will only get yourself—your ego, personality, self-limiting beliefs and judgments—out of the way.

I first experienced this when I was working overseas. In 1973, I was working for the High Commissioner of Refugees Office at the United Nations in Geneva, Switzerland. I was 23 years old at the time, and I was amazed at the diversity and richness of the world and people around me. This diversity contrasted sharply with the States, where we only seemed to hear news about our own nation and community and very little about the rest of the world. In Switzerland, the news covered the whole world, with only a small portion dealing with the United States.

My daily routines, and even the way I defined myself, were disrupted by the European pace of life and the challenges of a different language and culture. As a result, I prayed and meditated more than usual. My dream life also became vivid and compelling, offering insights about my relationship with my family, myself, and the world around me.

I had been recording my dreams for several months, spending my first hour each morning in either prayerful meditation or working with the content of my dreams. Gradually, I began to feel a stillness in my heart which I had rarely experienced. The world around me appeared more vibrant and colorful. When I went for my daily walks (also a new behavior) I felt the earth rising to support me, and I noticed the living power of nature as I remembered experiencing it as a child. I would "see" the bark of a tree, "hear" the song of a bird, and "feel" gentle breezes on my face, as well as a thousand other sensations I rarely noticed.

After I had been in Geneva for about six months, I woke up one morning from a dream in which I had been sobbing, feeling a tremendous longing. It was a dream of loss, of being left behind and feeling utterly alone and unloved. I felt a great ache in my heart that was overwhelming. But, realizing the dream was a gift of my soul, I prayed for the courage to embrace the longing and fully experience it.

I closed my eyes and opened up to the pain and longing. At first, the feelings intensified, but suddenly the intensity subsided to a dull ache. I soon found my mind filled with thoughts of breakfast and all the tasks that needed to be accomplished that day. Finally, I got up, dressed, ate breakfast, and went to work, where my mind was filled with all the duties I needed to perform. Immersed in the morning's work, I completely forgot the painful loneliness. In fact, my boss had to remind me to take a lunch break.

As I walked toward the cafeteria, I "woke up" from the spell of work and suddenly felt disoriented and alone again, my mind in turmoil and my heart full of pain. I stopped near the doors and looked at the people, who came from many different races and wore all manner of dress—some in saris, some in suits, others in turbans. As I stood there, I was blessed by grace, as if the hand of some angel had brushed my heart, and I was filled with an overflowing sense of love and a profound peace I had never felt before. Suddenly, everything seemed absolute-

ly right and natural. I felt I knew each person completely and perfectly, even though several hundred people
filled the room, many of whom I had never seen before.
Nevertheless I felt profound love for each person, knowing our lives were intimately connected. My heart was
filled with joy, love, gratitude, and peace. My whole
body vibrated with incredible energy.

I took a lunch tray and selected some soup and
yogurt, overjoyed by the touch of the containers, the
smell of the food, and the face of the cashier, who smiled
pleasantly as I paid her. As I walked to a table, everyone
seemed to look up, beaming with greetings and acknowl-
edging my presence in some way, whether by nodding or
speaking. They all smiled and seemed to drink in the
same contact I felt. It was a play of love and joy to be in
that room with all those wonderful and loving people.

The feeling lasted for about an hour. Then it slowly
faded, leaving me for the rest of the day and evening
with a sense of wonder and a profound feeling of gratitude. The experience changed my life, pointing me to a
career of exploring the depths of the human heart. It
also taught me that what I was seeking also sought me.
The key was to slow down and be "caught," to realize I
was, indeed, "the sought."

As I have worked with individuals, families, executives, and organizations in the past three decades, I find

that the greatest tragedy is the incredible loneliness, and the longing most people feel for a deeper connection with life. They search for a more loving connection to their parents, children, spouses, or God. This longing is often expressed simply, "I want to spend more time and share more of my life with . . ." The desire to know you are important, known, and loved, and to know that those you love feel your love and appreciation, is ultimately what is important. We feel a great hunger for love, longing for a more profound experience of being alive. It takes courage to face this longing and allow what we pursue to actually catch up with us.

In the Hasidic tradition, there is a story of a great rabbi who had many students. It came to pass that this Rabbi was dying. His students kept vigil around his deathbed to feel the comfort of his presence, and perhaps hear his last words of wisdom. One day, his students were startled to hear him cry out in fear about his imminent meeting with God. "But, Master," said one student, "what do you have to fear? You have the wisdom of Solomon!"

Another student spoke up, "Yes, and you have the courage of David."

Yet another student added, "And you have the moral integrity of Moses."

The old rabbi looked up at them and said, "Listen, I'm not afraid God will ask me why I wasn't a Solomon, or a David, or a Moses. I'm afraid He will ask me why I wasn't fully myself!"

Similarly, Rabbi Harold Kushner, author of *When Everything You Ever Wanted Isn't Enough*, says that as he has sat with powerful executives who were on their deathbeds, not one of them in their last hours wishes for more money, more fame, or more time to complete their projects. Instead, they express thoughts such as, "I wish I'd spent more time with my family," or "I wish I'd known my children better," or "I wish I'd taken the time to know who I am."

When I worked as a marital and family therapist, I used the *Diagnostic and Statistical Manual*, second edition, which describes all the diagnostic categories of emotional distress, psychological disorders, and mental illness using consistent terminology and descriptions for the many problems and complaints people have. Each diagnosis is found on a continuum: from mild to moderate to severe. After years of providing therapy, I developed my own diagnosis that seemed to account for just about every category of distress. I labeled the new category chronic lack of self-love. By labeling this as the foundational issue, I was able to have a powerful and helpful impact most of the time.

In the years since I developed that diagnostic category I have worked with thousands of people, many of them executives, and the diagnosis seems even more universal and useful than I first suspected. Every situation I have addressed, whether it was an individual, a family, or an organization, rested on the foundation of chronic lack of self-love, usually in the moderate range.

In one example, the CEO of a $200 million company faced ongoing conflicts with front-line employees because of the high turnover of senior managers. The organization seemed "spastic," with many starts and stops, as new executives brought in new initiatives and management styles. The CEO thought the problem was that he could not get people to implement his strategic vision. He saw the turnover as a sad but reasonable problem, since the company continued to grow in sales and profits.

But it became apparent that the CEO could not tolerate criticism. He wanted his direct reports to praise his ideas, and then to improve upon and execute them effectively. He insisted on hiring bright, competent, and aggressive managers who had been successful in other organizations. These executives did not view their functions as "rubber stamps" for his views. They expressed strong opinions and compelling insights, backed with logical analysis.

In a Leadership Impact Study conducted by my company, we challenged the CEO and the other senior executives to consider what behaviors they helped to create, perhaps unconsciously, through their actions. The study, along with anonymous feedback from the people impacted by his behavior, served as a wake-up call for the CEO. He began to see what had been getting in the organization's way. He felt a strong need to prove himself, to measure up, which was driven by insecurity. And, because of this need to prove himself, he had seen himself as the sole champion of the organization and had not made room for anyone else. Whenever he received critical feedback, he reacted as if he had been told he was wrong, and his defense was to prove himself right and the other person wrong. This pattern was destructive of his real intent. The core was a chronic lack of self-love, at the moderate end of the spectrum.

Gradually, the CEO improved, learning to make room for others and to hear critical feedback. He learned to address his need for love and approval in more conscious and effective ways. He developed the courage to be vulnerable, to allow himself to feel the respect and approval others felt for him without questioning their loyalty when they challenged his ideas. The organization improved dramatically and his leadership became more powerful as a result.

To let ourselves be vulnerable, to love and be loved, requires great courage. It means challenging self-limiting definitions, thoughts, feelings, and assumptions. We activate this courage by developing first five acts of courage: dreaming, seeing current reality, confronting, being confronted, and learning and growing. Still, the courage to be vulnerable and to love is different in kind. We must consciously choose to be open and vulnerable. Without vulnerability, we cannot experience true love, nor can we allow others to fully express their love.

Max DePree, retired CEO and chairman of the board at Herman Miller, expressed this well. When asked what he hoped to leave as his legacy, he said, "I want people to say of me, of us, that we were a gift to the spirit."

To be a gift to the spirit is to have the courage to be vulnerable, to love. To give this gift to our families, our organizations, and our society, is to remember that, ultimately, what we seek is also seeking us. We are the sought. We have the power to choose, each moment of our lives, to act with courage and to be more open and vulnerable. And our choices, moment by moment, shape us and affirm our presence in the world and the presence of those around us.

SUMMARY AND EXERCISES:

Developing the Courage to
Be Vulnerable, to Love

"You thought you were the seeker, and find you are the sought."

The courage to be vulnerable, to love, can be daunting. So many messages run counter to the whole concept of vulnerability: "Be strong," "Never give in," "Be independent," "Keep your guard up," "Play your cards close to the vest," "Don't appear weak or vulnerable," "Don't trust anyone," and so forth.

First: Choose love. Consciously choose to be vulnerable. Realize that the best defense lies in being defenseless. Let go of the need to defend yourself or your point of view. Instead, look deep into your heart and the heart of others. Practice and play with the thought, "What I am seeking is also seeking me."

• Practice letting go of judgment. To judge is to separate yourself from life and from others. Instead, learn to be curious, to inquire and seek deeper understanding.

• Remember your dream, what you most wish to create; remind yourself of what you most deeply desire. Affirm that dream and choose it again, out loud.

• Write out what you most want and what you would need for you to become open if you are to obtain it. What do you need to let go of or surrender to obtain it?

• Look deeply at those you live and work with, as well as those around you. Open yourself up to their gifts, talents, and abilities. They may help you in ways you had not considered.

• Consider the concept of "tough love." Accept no excuses for failure to achieve the results required for success, yet always maintain compassion in interacting with others. Care about the person, but be tough on goals and required results.

Second: Practice letting go. Mentally rehearse opening up. Share your heartfelt feelings with others. Look deeply into the hearts of those around you to sense their needs.

• Allow yourself to explore your deepest longing, loneliness, or sorrow. Find a picture of yourself as a little child that touches the longing or compassion within you for the child in the picture. Place the picture on the mirror in your bathroom. Look into the child's eyes and notice what you feel. Offer your love and appreciation to that child. Speak out loud, saying, "I love you, and you deserve to be loved and appreciated. I will take care of you, cherish you, and help you grow and thrive."

• Grieve for what you have missed or never had. List the things you feel you have missed out on, or wanted but didn't experience. Be specific. Focus particularly on key relationships in your childhood and teenage years. Write a letter to yourself to express the grief, sorrow, or regret you feel. Allow yourself to mourn the loss.

• Pray, meditate, write in your journal, and examine your dreams. Invite your dream life to inform you about your inner life. Open yourself up to guidance from the soul. Allow the loving images, dreams, and thoughts that come to you to blossom. Write them in your journal. Draw a picture or series of pictures. Create a collage of the images that captures your feelings. Place the collage in a prominent place in your home for a few weeks and then create a new one, noticing what has changed and come to life within you.

• Imagine you are the sought, the beloved; imagine the world reaching out to you. Imagine yourself taking the world in your arms. As you breathe in, feel the light and air rushing in to fill you. Notice how the ground supports you, how the world rises to meet you and take care of you. Understand that you are the sought, and that a living spirit seeks to fill you.

• Care for your heart. Imagine yourself going to the center of your heart. Imagine you see, at the center of your heart, an image of what you most love. Breathe in and out, imagining that the image lives because of your breath and fills your heart. Breathe into the space around you. Feel your heart expanding to fill the space. Breathe in and out from your heart, imagining you feel and see the image filling the space around you. Imagine as you breathe that the image fills the entire building, penetrates the ground, and fills the air above the building. See and feel the image of what you most deeply love. Feel your capacity to love expand. Feel the world filling your heart and your heart containing the world. You are the sought, the beloved, the loving.

• Practice silently blessing the different people you meet during the day. Pay particular attention to those who are struggling or people you normally would complain about. Send a silent blessing instead. Notice what happens to your inner feelings as you do this over several days.

• Commit to having the courage to be vulnerable, to love. Notice the choices you make each day and each moment: to be open and loving, or to be protective and defensive.

THE SEVENTH ACT

THE COURAGE TO ACT

"Sing a song of glory, and you'll be that glory;
Naught are you but song, and as you sing you are."

The courage to act is, ultimately, what the other six acts point to in your life. When it comes down to it, will you have the courage to act, to put yourself on the line? The courage to act is the willingness to place yourself in "harm's way." To act requires the courage to leave the safety of being a spectator and to enter the arena. It requires the courage to commit yourself and your heart, and to enter a profound relationship with life.

The courage to act drives the other six acts of courage (to dream and put forth that dream, to see current reality, to confront, to be confronted, to learn and grow, and to be vulnerable, to love). However, the other acts empower, support, inform, and direct the courage to act. Without them, we act in a vacuum, answering only the insistent, automatic calls of our ego and our comfort zone. But without the power to act, we lack the ability to move.

Carpe diem, seize the day, is the motto of those who cultivate the courage to act. Courageous action requires a full commitment of time, energy, effort, and the willingness to risk your ego. Until we act on what we believe and know, and express what is in our hearts, we merely observe life instead of living it. The courage to act, married to the other acts of courage, is the mark of wholehearted living, and it forms a profound relationship with the soul.

In the wonderful Earth Sea trilogy by award-winning author Ursula K. LeGuin, a young wizard named Ged learns about the courage of facing his fears and taking meaningful action. In the first book, *A Wizard of Earth Sea*, Ged uses his magic to call up a spirit of the dead. In doing so, he lets loose on the world a demon from a different dimension. The creature wounds him, but Ged's life is saved and the demon is driven off. Ged sets out to find his place in the world, bearing in his face the scars from the dark night when he faced the demon.

Out in the world, the young wizard finds he is being stalked by the demon. He flees in terror, turning himself into a hawk and flying to the home of Ogion the Mage, a former mentor whom he asks for protection. Ogion listens to Ged's predicament and then tells him that the demon will eventually destroy him if he continues to run from it. "These things," he tells Ged, "feed on your fears." By running, Ged will only destroy himself. Ged argues that running is the only thing he can do, but Ogion encourages a confrontation and then goes to bed. The next morning, when Ogion awakens, he finds a message: "Master, I have gone hunting."

When Ged pursues the demon that has been pursuing him, it flees. Later, after chasing the demon through different lands, he corners it. As the two come together, Ged sees that the demon is an exact replica of himself. Thus, by having the courage to act in spite of his fears, the young wizard becomes able to integrate a wilder, unknown part of himself, and gain power and wisdom.

Facing what we fear, to act rather than react, requires courage. It requires the courage to act in spite of doubts, obstacles, fears, or past disappointments and failures.

When my father retired from the military, he threw his heart into a real estate insurance business, which hinged on the financing of a wealthy friend. Within six months, he had created millions of dollars in profits for the company and generated several hundred thousand dollars in commissions for himself—more money than he'd made in the previous three years combined. Although he was elated, the commission checks did not arrive as scheduled. He called the insurance underwriters, who assured him the checks would come shortly.

Six months later, as he sat at his desk, six men from the FBI came into his office. They escorted my father and two other employees into the conference room, where four other agents surrounded the company president, "Ron Gordon." The FBI had been monitoring Gordon and had held up the checks from the underwriters.

A former insider to a mafia Don, Gordon had left the mob and had stolen a substantial amount of money from his former associates. He had changed his name to avoid detection and had used the stolen money to set up a legitimate business. The FBI informed Gordon that the mob had recently placed a contract on his head. The business was closed down, having been started with stolen money, and all proceeds were held or confiscated. My father and the two employees were released, having done nothing wrong, but Gordon was placed in the witness protection program. Everyone was to return home, forget about Gordon, and pick up their lives without contacting any company clients.

My father was shocked that the man he had trusted was not who he seemed, and that all he thought he had earned was being taken away. As the FBI rummaged through his office, my father returned home, now facing the lowest point in his life. Eventually, my father was allowed to see Gordon one more time, under agent supervision, to say good-bye. He asked his friend why he had lied to him; Gordon answered that he had simply wanted to start his life over with his family. He then apologized, and the two men parted.

For three days, my father remained at home in his room. He seemed to have given up hope. Neither World War II, nor the Korean War, nor other losses or hard knocks had ever beaten him and his "can do" attitude. But one con man who tried to go straight had apparently sunk the unsinkable. Dad appeared utterly defeated.

On the third day, he got up, looked at my mom, and said, "I don't know what will happen, but I can at least take action to make a new beginning." He went out and began to sell again, and, over the next five years, created a new company. He later told me that the love of his family was what had allowed him to move forward in the face of betrayal, business failure, huge debts, and financial loss. He said, "I didn't want you to think it was okay to just give up. We all owe more to our families than the easy way out, even though sometimes it's tempting to just give up." He had found, once again, the courage to act. A lifetime of challenges enabled him to rise from his crushing disappointment and start over.

The courage to act is the willingness to commit yourself and to move on what is in front of you instead of bewailing what was, or dreaming of what might have been. It is the bold, brazen act of stepping forward and seizing your life. It is taking the opportunity to create your life in the moment, regardless of what you face. It is moving in the face of fear and the specter of defeat and loss.

During the battle of Gettysburg, the Army of the Potomac, over 100,000 strong, faced the 70,000-man Army of Northern Virginia. The Union army had suffered many defeats at the hands of General Robert E. Lee and his brilliant commanders, General "Stonewall" Jackson and General Longstreet. Newly appointed Union commander General Meade held the high ground near the town of Gettysburg, while Colonel Joshua Lawrence Chamberlain held the flank position of the Union line.

On the first day of the battle, July 1, 1863, Confederate forces drove Union forces out of the town and seemed to prevail. On the second day, Lee intended to flank the entrenched Union forces by taking the small hill called "Little Round Top," where Colonel Chamberlain was positioned. Chamberlain was told he could not retreat; he was to "hold the position to the last." During the long afternoon, Chamberlain's forces held their ground, repulsing multiple attacks by some of the best soldiers in the Confederacy under General

Hood. By evening, Chamberlain's command had been reduced to less than 200 men, and most were out of ammunition. The hard-pressed Union army had been unable to provide reinforcements or supplies.

As Chamberlain looked down the sloping hill at the Confederate forces mounting yet another attack, he knew if he stood his ground with little or no ammunition that his line would be overwhelmed and would fail. He also knew that if he retreated, Confederate forces would sweep up the hill and outflank the Union army, which would then lose the battle and possibly the War.

In an instant, he sized up his options and selected the one plan that was most improbable and also most direct. Stepping to the front, he shouted, "Bayonets!" His 200 men affixed their bayonets and followed him in a charge down the hill toward some 500 fully armed Confederate soldiers who were attacking Chamberlain's position. But the frenzied attack, and the surprise of Chamberlain's action, stunned the Confederate forces, many of whom turned to run; and Chamberlain's small, poorly armed force saved the battle for the Union.

Certain defeat was turned into victory by Chamberlain's courage to act. His courage came both from conviction and from the prior examination of his soul. He acted from self-awareness, practiced study, and confidence about what he and the Union army were about.

As I mentioned earlier, the courage to act is actually derived from the other six acts of courage. Without the first six acts, we ultimately have no sustainable capacity to take meaningful action. Yet, without the courage to take action, the other six acts remain fruitless.

1. *The courage to dream and put forth that dream.* My father and Colonel Chamberlain both had dreams about what they wanted to create, and they put forth their dreams to all who would listen. Without the boldness of a dream, of a larger purpose to our lives and work, we lack inspiration and direction.

2. *The courage to see current reality.* Both my father and Chamberlain had no illusions that their tasks would be easy; they saw current reality and the peril within it. They realized their resources had been spent, yet they still faced the stark options before them. Without the courage to see current reality, we remain unaware of what we face and what we have to work with, as well as ignorant of how to go about our work most effectively. Telling the truth to ourselves and others about where we stand, and about what we are standing for, is crucial in gaining the traction to move toward our goals.

3. *The courage to confront.* Both men were willing to confront the people around them with the truth of the situation, and both confronted the situation itself. Without the courage to confront we cannot assert ourselves in the world, nor can we claim our power. Instead, we live lives of partial paralysis as we resist expressing ourselves.

4. *The courage to be confronted.* The two men were willing to hear the truth from others and to avoid the pitfalls of wishful thinking or denial. If we do not listen to others or allow ourselves to be confronted by the truth, then we are at the mercy of forces we cannot see or acknowledge, vulnerable to failure, and blind to greater effectiveness.

5. *The courage to learn and grow.* Both men were lifelong students of their chosen professions and of life itself. They studied, read, thought, and put into practice many new behaviors and ideas, stretching and preparing themselves to handle whatever challenges might come, with courage and competence. When we lack the courage to learn and grow, to give up our addiction to being "right," we do not learn quickly or effectively; we do not adapt to new circumstances, and we fall behind.

6. *The courage to be vulnerable, to love.* Both Chamberlain and my father opened their hearts to the people with whom they worked, and listened to their thoughts and feelings. They were sustained by the love and support they received from others, and could inspire others by touching their hearts. When we do not allow ourselves to be vulnerable or to feel the love and needs of others we develop dry and brittle souls. We deprive those around us and ourselves of the greatest gift we have to give: the gift of giving and receiving genuine appreciation, caring, and love.

7. The courage to act. Predisposed to act, and prepared to act by a lifetime of countless small choices to deal with what was before them, my father and Colonel Chamberlain both were ready to act when crises and challenges arose. In fact, the small choices became significant choices, since the smaller choices prepared the men's minds and toned their hearts for the larger encounters. This act of courage is the defining act, since all acts of courage ultimately rest upon our willingness to take action and to commit ourselves to a course. Without this act, we merely rehearse for life and never really live it.

What we act on and how we take action ultimately determine who we become in life. Our lives are woven from the day-to-day choices we make about the things we will and will not act upon. The courage to act means that whenever you sense a challenge in your life or work, you must move to understand and address it. Move toward the challenge, not away from it. Learning to move toward the challenges in your life is to cultivate the courage to act, as opposed to re-act. It is the choice to seize the moment, to seize the day. Through action, whether we are pursuing what we desire or addressing challenges before us, we shape ourselves and our lives.

All our acts of courage will come to nothing unless we have the courage to act on the truth as we see it and to pursue what we most desire. This act of courage is developed through commitment, discipline, intimacy, and focus.

Mother Teresa, considered by many a modern-day saint, was relentless in this particular act of courage. She had little regard for authority, for titles, for egos, for the past, or for excuses. She always found the courage to act in the moment and confront whatever was in front of her, occasionally deferring, only slightly, to the Pope. She was predisposed to act with integrity and full commitment, speaking always on behalf of the poorest of the poor.

Her whole life was based on courage, built by countless acts of courage. She found the courage to leave her family and commit to being a nun. She had the courage to leave her country for her mission in an Indian convent. Then, responding to an even deeper call, she had the courage to leave the safety of the convent to live and work in the streets of Calcutta.

Each act of courage developed her capacity to perform even greater acts. Her whole life was shaped by her courageous choices and actions.

The courage to act is the power we all have to shape our world by shaping ourselves. Each action, or inaction, helps to form our consciousness, our future behavior, our lives. In fact, modern science indicates that our very biology, the biochemical processes that keep us alive, is impacted by our thoughts and feelings, and thus, by the choices we make.

Dr. Candace Pert, the researcher who discovered pheromones, also discovered neuropeptides, the molecules that influence our biochemical processes and our nervous systems. Consequently, neuropeptides are closely connected to how we think and feel. Her research shows that whenever we have a thought, an emotion, or make a decision, we produce these molecules. These neuropeptides then act like keys, unlocking key reactions in both the brain and the cells of the body, such as the immune system. Her research has led to a new medical science, psychoneuroimmunology.

Simply put, we are what we think. More accurately, what we consistently think is what we eventually become or accomplish. Our choices, and the thoughts we entertain, impact how our mind and body function;

in fact, they actually shape our mind and body. What we choose affects the chemistry of our brain and body.

We have the power of choice: to act, think, feel, express ourselves, and interact in ways we see fit. This power not only requires courage, it requires knowledge and practice—it is not simply a matter of taking the "path of least resistance." The courage to act—to choose, to move beyond fears, doubts, comforts, old ways of thinking, and the resistance of others—is the pivotal act of courage that will allow us to live our lives wholeheartedly.

SUMMARY AND EXERCISES:

The Courage to Act

"Sing a song of glory, and you'll be that glory;
Naught are you but song, and as you sing you are."

The courage to act is the willingness to "sing our song of glory" and realize that "as we sing we are." How we choose to "sing" determines who we are, today and, increasingly, tomorrow. Each act shapes our lives. We live more wholeheartedly when we act with courage. It is through our acts of courage that we experience joy.

Prepare yourself to give traction to your dreams and aspirations. Great power may be found in seemingly small actions, such as writing down our commitments and dreams. A power is unleashed within our souls when we consciously choose our thoughts by directing toward what we can do and what we would like to experience. We can also find potent "magic" in using the imaginative power of our souls to create and apply helpful images in working with the deeper, nonverbal parts of who we are. We can act courageously by simply using imagination, perhaps coupled with drawing, writing, or the spoken word, to shape our interior landscape as we prepare to act in the larger world of family, friends, organizations, and society.

First: Resolve to face yourself. Know that what you don't face today will continue to drive you and shape you into something you may regret. Resolve to move toward the conflict. Act by facing what frightens you, what you are resisting, and what you have historically stumbled over.

• Look at the exercises from previous chapters, especially the courage to see current reality. Review your journal entries to look for patterns or themes that point to what trips you up.

• What do you most resist looking at in your own life? What internal "demons" (things you deny or don't want to see; conflicts or problems you face) are you running away from? What have you been avoiding or neglecting? A good clue can be found in things people say that irritate you. Notice your reactions to others. What irritates you or upsets you may indicate something below the surface of your ego.

• List two or three major issues—behaviors, recurring anxieties and fears, relationship conflicts at work or home, or other sources of pain—that impact your life.

• Resolve to "own" the patterns and to act on the knowledge that the patterns are yours and within your power to change.

• See yourself as having the courage to act on your life, both personally and professionally, as well as on your attitudes and self-limiting beliefs that may be problematic or off-purpose for who you are and what you wish to create.

Second: Remember, what you choose, every thought or decision, has consequences—not only at the social level, but also on the molecular level in your body, in its immune system and brain functions. What you think and choose shapes your biology and your unique human destiny.

• Review your journal to understand your thoughts, choices, and decisions. What would you change about how you have shaped your biology and your destiny? List the changes you would make.

• Make sure the list corresponds with what you most deeply desire and want to experience. (Review your dreams from the first chapter.) Select two or three of the most critical choices which would best move you toward your aspirations.

• Consciously choose the list. For example, "I choose to experience myself as loved and loving," or "I choose to face my fear of rejection by speaking my truth," or "I choose to express my love instead of holding it inside." Speak your choice out loud.

• Visualize yourself acting with courage in life. Create a collage or draw a picture of the ways you will be acting and living. Depict in images the choices you have made and will be making.

• Invite your soul to speak to you through dreams, inspiration, images from the natural world, or other synchronicity such as in songs you hear or books that come into your hands, or a "chance" meeting or conversation. Choose to be receptive to inspiration and messages of guidance and encouragement, along with other tools and resources. Choose to have a deeper and more intimate relationship with Creation and with your soul.

• See each day as a quest for developing your courage muscles and shaping your life and the world around you. Choose your deepest intention and remind yourself that you are shaping the rest of your life by every action and choice: by what you do and don't do, what you say and don't say, and by what you think and dwell upon.

• Claim your life. Act on what you most want to create. Choose to act today from the center of who you are.

CONCLUSION

LIVING OUR LIVES WHOLEHEARTEDLY

Sing a song of glory, and you'll be that glory;
Naught are you but song, and as you sing you are.

You thought you were the teacher, and find you are the taught;
You thought you were the seeker, and find you are the sought.

Sing a song of glory, and you'll be that glory;
Naught are you but song, and as you sing, you are.

—Sufi Chant

The 7 Acts of Courage represent a larger unifying process of living our lives with integrity, meaning, and power. This complex process may best be understood by separating the distinct forms of courage required for living a wholehearted life. We can shape a life in which joy is frequent by learning to discern which act of courage is required and then learning how to engage that act. We can develop our capacity to act wisely and courageously by first identifying which act is needed and then practicing that act both in our imagination and our lives.

I compare the 7 Acts of Courage to the seven cardinal directions held sacred by the Native American tribes. They provide orientation and direction on how to live full and wholehearted lives, regardless of the circumstances. They offer clear choices and actions to empower your life and to observe and understand the world. They also point to where the powers to learn, to grow, and to act with wisdom and compassion in any situation may be found. To me, the seven sacred directions are more helpful and profound than our four points of the compass, based on a two-dimensional model. As Native American tribes realized, a more complete set of directions includes:

- North
- South
- East
- West
- Up
- Down
- Within

These directions, applied to courage, are guides to a well-rounded and wholehearted way of life. They lead to a richer way of expressing your gifts to the world around you. Just as we need the four cardinal points of the map, and the vertical dimension that includes up and down, we also need the dimension of the soul, within, if we are to live with mastery, depth, and fulfillment. In this setting, courage is appropriately applied to the seven cardinal points. Just as the seven directions offer guidance and direction to those who honor and follow them, so too, the 7 Acts of Courage give us a profound means of orienting, guiding, and inspiring us.

North: The Courage to Dream and Put Forth That Dream

North has historically been the direction for orienting people on the earth to go "True North," just as the courage to dream and put forth that dream is our orientation and guidance to our own destiny. In Native American traditions, north is the direction of wisdom, the deep, guiding wisdom of our inner spirit that reminds us of our deepest aspirations.

A 67-year-old woman had a dream for herself. After she had raised eight children, she decided she wanted to obtain a college degree and become a journalist. Her grown children tried to talk her out of this "fantasy," but she was stubborn. Over the next ten years, she took courses here and there and finally earned her degree at age 77. She landed a job writing political commentary for the local newspaper! Clearly, this woman had the courage to dream and put forth her dream to the world. She had the courage to orient herself and follow her star.

South: The Courage to See Current Reality

South is traditionally the direction of warmth, of touching the earth and being grounded. It is the opposite of North, which represents dreams. To the south is heat, or pressure, in opposition to the dream. It represents what stands in the way of our dreams, but it also represents the ground on which we stand.

A young mother of two felt depressed and overwhelmed. She shared her pain about the lack of love she felt from her husband, and how distant he had become. He completely ignored her sexually, and she was afraid of what it might mean. I asked if she could step back and be the compassionate, observing friend to herself in the situation, as she had been to so many others. When she heard this, her mouth dropped open and she exclaimed, "He's having an affair and doesn't have the guts to tell me. He is lying to himself and me." In that moment, she found the courage to see the truth she had been avoiding. She now saw her relationship with her husband in a new light. She then engaged another act of courage by confronting him, and, in the process, shaped a new life for her family. But she never would have been able to act if she had continued to avoid seeing current reality.

East: The Courage to Confront

East is the direction of illumination. It represents enlightenment through speaking up and confronting the people and situations you face. It is the direction of the sunrise, casting light on your own self-expression. Confrontation can be brilliant: "sparks" fly and they illuminate not only the people or situations we confront, but the soul itself.

A woman climbed onto the local bus and sat in an empty seat behind the bus driver. The driver turned to her and said, "Lady, move to the back!" But she just sat there. "Lady, you know where you belong; move to the back, now!" Some of the passengers glared at her; others looked away. But her feet were tired that day, and she was tired of the discrimination and prejudice.

That day, Rosa Parks made history, finding in herself the courage to confront the tyranny of prejudice and racism through the simple act of sitting where she wanted, rather than the back of the bus where people of color had been relegated. She proved to be one of the most visible sparks in igniting the civil rights movement. Her courage to confront a corrupt system and social order based on prejudice and intimidation came from the depths of who she was. She challenged the status quo, enduring ridicule and threats in the process.

West: The Courage to Be Confronted

West is the direction of reflection and introspection. It represents the willingness to be confronted, to reflect on what comes to you as judgments, criticisms, and confrontations. In the heart, we either allow ourselves to hear others and their messages, or we get lost in the labyrinth of our own thoughts.

An executive stood up in a seminar, struggling with his anger. He had played professional football and still showed great physical power. He towered over the woman who faced him. "I don't have to listen to this!" he said loudly.

The woman smiled back, undaunted, and replied, "No, you don't need to listen. You can turn a deaf ear if you want. Only you, and those who live with you, still have to pay the price. Do you really want me to shut up?"

The big man grimaced, but found the courage to ask, "What do you mean? What 'price'?"

The facilitator met his gaze and gently asked, "What about peace? Does your anger leave a wake in your life which is less than peaceful? Does it hurt you and those around you?"

The man visibly slumped as her kind tone penetrated his heart. "Yeah, I pay a price," he said. "I don't like the way I yell at my kids. It's hard to relax. In fact, . . ." he paused and looked at her with pain in his eyes, "I don't enjoy my life very much." Then he took the next step, which took him deeper into the courage to be confronted: "Tell me what you see," he invited her. "I want to know how to break this pattern of rage."

He took a hard look at how he had constructed his defenses. He was open to seeing how his anger toward his father, who had left him and his mother when he was only eleven, had contaminated his whole life. Despite his success in football and business, he was not able to enjoy it and seemed perpetually irritated or angry with people around him. Over the next few days, he considered his life and the choices he had made which were less than fulfilling.

On the last day of the seminar he came into the classroom radiating energy. "I just talked to my father last night for the first time in over 25 years," he said. "He was glad to hear from me. I told him I wanted to get to know him, and for him to get to know me, before it was too late. It's like some huge grinding-wheel inside my gut has finally stopped."

By having the courage to be confronted, this giant of a man stepped out of the constricted heart space he had created and, for the first time, stood up to his full spiritual height.

Up: The Courage to Learn and Grow

Up is the direction we grow, toward the light. It is a symbol of higher power, spirituality, and growth. It represents learning about ourselves, about life, and about how to live life, as well as the courage to be students again. It means letting go of the hard casing of what is known, like a seed, and opening up to new possibilities and growth.

My grandmother, Marcie Haynes, felt completely overwhelmed. Her husband had become completely bedridden, slowly dying from diabetes. She still had five children at home to support, the last a pre-teenager. She felt the weight of caring for her beloved spouse, while she raised the children and, somehow, earned a living.

Marcie had been through trials and challenges before. She had been married at the age of 14 to a man in his thirties, and she'd had seven children by him before she was 28. Her husband abandoned the family, and she had supported herself and the children working as a housekeeper. Then, in her early thirties, she married the man who touched her heart, and they had three more children. They loved each other deeply. Now she watched him, bedridden, sick, and wasting away, and, despite her pain and breaking heart, she still had the rest of the family to support. She sought his help on how to care for the family's needs. She needed a job that would bring more income but that would allow her to spend time with her husband and the three youngest children.

"Marcie, my love," grandfather said, "you love children. You have a knack for calming people down. Why not become a midwife and help bring new lives into the world?" She shuddered and debated with him from her fear. She objected that she didn't know enough, that she hadn't finished school, that she might hurt someone, that she didn't have the ability, and that she wasn't smart enough. After she ran down a bit, he smiled and said, "Funny thing, you've helped deliver three children for other people, and one of them you delivered before the doctor even arrived. All he did was wave his hands and pronounce that it was a healthy baby." As she started to object again, he interrupted, "Besides, you've had ten children of your own. That makes you a 'certified expert' on the subject. If you could do that, you can do anything."

She found the courage to study with a midwife, and soon overcame the fear that she wasn't going to be smart enough. In the following years, my grandmother delivered over 300 babies, all healthy except for one stillbirth. She also supported her family and cared for her husband. My grandmother had shown the courage to learn and to grow, moving into the world as a midwife and provider for her family.

Down: The Courage to Be Vulnerable, to Love

Down is the direction of humility, of planting and digging, and of putting down roots. It represents the vitality of what sustains us. It is where we penetrate the surface of our being and realize that what we most desire, what we most seek, also seeks us; that we are the sought.

A colleague of mine, a gifted consultant and trainer, had just returned from an out-of-town business trip. It was Halloween, and as she drove up to her house the neighborhood was filled with parents and children in costumes. She had no candy, and she also believed Halloween was a nuisance and wanted no part of it. She put her car in the garage and slipped into the house, lighting only a candle, hoping no one would come to the door.

She was irritated with the world and with herself for slinking about her house in the dark. Children rang the doorbell several times while she remained still, trying not to make a sound. But finally, after the fourth ring, she turned the lights on and answered the door, ready to admit she was home. She saw a little girl dressed as a fairy and a little boy dressed as a monster. "I'm very sorry," she explained, "I just got home from a trip, and I don't have any candy." She waited for the confrontation, or anger, or disappointment in their faces.

Instead, the little girl just looked up and smiled, "That's okay, I can help you." The little girl reached into her bag and lifted out three big handfuls of candy, giving them to her. "Now, you have lots of candy to give other children," she said.

"You really are a fairy godmother, aren't you?" marveled my friend.

The little girl beamed and replied, "Yes, I am." And the two turned and marched off.

My friend found the courage to be vulnerable. She spoke from her vulnerability and found an incredible gift of love flowing back to her. She felt she had become the sought, receiving love and a lesson in generosity from a little "fairy godmother" just when she needed it.

Within: The Courage to Act

Within is the direction of the soul and of mystery, of depth and personal mastery. It represents the inner wisdom to know when and how to act, to have the courage to act as needed in small, everyday matters, as well as in large, life-changing events. It also represents the essence of who we are, moving into the world with authority and power even when we feel scared and doubtful. For, in the act itself, we transcend our fears, doubts, egos, and personal limitations.

My father was stationed in Korea on a second tour of duty after the end of the conflict. One evening, just after midnight, he awoke in his tent to the sound of rushing water and pouring rain. He sat up and looked at his watch; it took him a moment to realize he was hearing another sound, above the wind, rain, and rushing water: the sound of children screaming.

He rolled out of his cot and rushed into the rain. In his sleepiness, he thought his children were screaming; but the cold rain hit him with a start, and he realized the screams came from a village near the small hill where his unit was camped. As he walked to the edge of the hill, the roar of water became louder, and he saw a dark, rushing wall of water smashing through what had been the center of the village. He ran back toward the camp, calling to the other men in the company. Flashlights came on and sleepy men made their way to the side of the hill. Their flashlights revealed adults and children clinging to poles, formerly huts, in the middle of the rushing water. Other families stood on shaking roofs half covered by water. A few adults and children had reached higher ground and were shouting to the people in the water, and then to the soldiers when they saw the flashlights.

My father, dragging every bit of rope he could find, came rushing back. He began frantically tying knots in the ropes. Several men began to help, tying lengths together. The rest backed away. My father, terrified for the safety of the children, began shouting orders. Several of the men argued with him, above the noise, shouting things like, "There's nothing we can do!" "You can't order us to commit suicide!" "It's impossible to help them. Let's call for help!"

My father looked at the men helping with the ropes, and then at the two dozen men huddled together in indecision. He stepped closer to the men and said, "I can hear the voices of my own children crying, and they sound the same. Can't you hear? What if they were your children? Your wives? Will you help me?" Finally, all the men participated in the rescue, and more than three-fourths of the village was saved.

Consider the stories and examples in this book and the stories in your own life that have touched you, shaped you, and guided you. They are living illustrations of courage, pointing to something larger and more enlivening in our souls. Whether the acts are large or small, they predispose us to act with even more courage later on. We develop our "courage muscle," the heart, every time we face our fears, doubts, or anxieties and act with integrity. Collectively, the 7 Acts of Courage form a tapestry that reveals the living spirit in our lives and helps us embrace a more wholehearted and joyful life.

Personally, I am uplifted and amazed when I reflect on who we are. Each of us is a vast mystery. No one except God can encompass, let alone comprehend, our true nature. Ultimately, like God, we are unknowable, continually unfolding our mystery every day of our lives. The creative intelligence in our minds is awesome. We are a vital part of the universe, and our actions, thoughts, words, and deeds make a difference. It really matters what we think, and our thoughts impact the world around us. At the very least, our thoughts shape our attitudes, beliefs, and feelings, which in turn shape our actions, our words, and our lives.

Earl Nightingale said that the thought which shaped and liberated his life was a sentence he discovered when he was in his early twenties: "As you think, so you are." I would add the theme of this book: "Sing a song of glory, and you'll be that glory." The truth is "As you act, so you become." Our acts of courage, then, shape our relationships and the world around us.

May we live each day of our lives with the courage to live wholeheartedly and find success, fulfillment, joy, and love.

ABOUT THE AUTHOR

Robert E. "Dusty" Staub, II is Chairman/CEO and founded Staub Leadership Solutions. He has spent more than 29 years working with individuals, organizations, families and community groups to deliver effective coaching in personal and organizational leadership development. In the past 12 years, thousands of executives have gone through his intensive Helping Individuals Lead Successfully (HILS) seminar. Dusty is the author of *The Heart of Leadership*, and his material has been published or cited in many national publications, including *Fortune*, *Reader's Digest*, *Executive Excellence*, *The Business Journal* and *LeaderQuest*.

Dusty is married to Dr. Christine Staub, MD, a family medicine practitioner. The couple resides in Kernersville, North Carolina. They have three children: Sean, Kendra and Chamberlain. Dusty's interests include reading anything and everything, spending time with his children, taking long walks in the woods, and yoga.

You may contact Dusty via e-mail at dusty@staubleadership.com or call (336) 282-0282.

About Staub Leadership Solutions

Staub Leadership Solutions is a comprehensive leadership development organization dedicated to helping its clients achieve personal and organizational effectiveness through improved leadership, empowerment, communications, and team-based creativity. The firm's approach is unique in that it combines elements of behavioral science with business-based practices to provide enduring solutions. The company partners with organizations across the spectrum of U.S. industry, ranging from Fortune 500 companies to mid-size and small companies, helping their partners to master the challenges of leadership and achieve bottom-line results.

Standard Programs:
- Helping Individuals Lead Successfully
- Enabling Change
- The Heart of Leadership Mastery
- Strategic Leadership Life Plan
- Matrix Management

Customized Packages:
- Team-Based Creativity
- Team Development
- Leadership Development
- Individual Executive Development/Coaching
- Climate Studies
- Facilitation Training
- Leadership Intensive Trainings
- 360-Degree Assessments
- Keynote Speeches

The company offers a wide array of customized and tailored packages and processes that can benefit you or your organization.

For more information about our products and programs from Staub Leadership Solutions, please contact:

Staub Leadership Solutions
166B Thatcher Rd.
Greensboro, NC 27409
Phone: (336) 282-0282
Fax: (336) 282-6013
Web: www.staubleadership.com

Books of Related Interest from Staub Leadership Solutions:

ROBERT E. STAUB II
The Heart of Leadership

Robert "Dusty" Staub tells us that those who purport to lead often fail because they don't understand who it is they're trying to be; they don't know how to lead. Dusty teaches us about the four chambers that make up the heart of a true leader: competency, intimacy, integrity, and passion.

To order this book, call (336) 282-0282